THE FLICKS

CKS

or whatever became of Andy Hardy?

by Charles Champlin

Ward Ritchie Press · Pasadena, California

This book was designed by Einar Vinje

Contents

Preface

When I first came to Hollywood in 1959 the industry was in a state of crisis. Actually the industry is always in a state of crisis, although some states are more critical than others.

In 1959, however, the crisis was genuine. Twentieth Century-Fox, for example, was teetering at the edge of bankruptcy, the sprawling studio maintained by a skeleton crew of a hundred workers. A photographer caught a picture of some of the jackrabbits that were the principal occupants of the back lot.

The movie audience was contracting even faster than the television audience was growing and the major studios—some of them with leadership problems and not at executive best—were trying desperately to get along in a radically different and uncomfortable age.

Still it seemed to me that the movies, even in disarray, were fascinating, important and powerful, influencing the lives of all of us, as they always had. I had asked George Hunt, then the managing editor of *Life*, to let me exchange the tyranny of the New York Central timetable for the thrills of the freeways, and he kindly obliged me.

I watched Hollywood while reporting mountain rescues and murders, politics and other disasters. Occasionally I had a chance to report on Hollywood itself—a Writers Guild strike, a story on a beautiful, intelligent and unknown newcomer named Yvette Mimieux. I wasn't sorry I had come west and I began to sense that the movies had learned something from the theater about how to be a fabulous invalid, thriving on reports of its own terminal ailments.

After watching Fox survive its crisis (or that crisis) thanks to Darryl Zanuck and *The Longest Day,* I went to London for three years to report on the movies and all the other arts for *Time.* Luckily those were the years of swinging London (swinging Britain, really) but it was before *Time* broke the spell by celebrating the scene in a cover piece.

Since 1965 I've been writing about the movies and the men, women and children who make them, for the *Los Angeles Times* and since 1967 I've been reviewing movies as well.

I'm not sure how many states of crisis there have been in that time; they tend to blur together. But during those years movie-going bottomed out and has started to climb back. The movies have lost whatever lingering inhibitions they had in 1965 and now enjoy (although that is not always the right word) virtually total freedom of expression. At many studios the executive suites needed revolving doors, as yesterday's boss became today's independent producer (although admittedly often by preference).

Every generation since 1896 has grown up with the movies, but my generation grew up with the movies and without television. The movies entertained us, inspired us, consoled us, shaped us profoundly; taught us (although not invariably wisely or well) and attempted to spare us from certain bitter truths about the world.

Their view of the world was positive and optimistic. But now, because what the movies say of the world is no longer always positive or optimistic or reassuring, many of my generation and older generations feel a kind of betrayal, an abandonment that has led many of them to abandon the movies in return.

A writer contemplating the armloads of film books already in existence thinks hard about committing another. Yet the great majority fall into two groupings. On one side are the fan works, nostalgic and worshipful, retrieving the past and finding that whatever was must have been wonderful. On the other side are the scholarly works of film history and film analysis, addressed to limited, specialist audiences.

Somewhere, I think, there is a middle ground, for those who, let's say, are able to remember Carmen Miranda without idolizing her (I cite that amusing performer only because she is the object of a small but vivid cult). It is, more broadly speaking, an audience of those who, having grown up with the movies, are interested in and possibly even fascinated by them, who read all the reviews but go to the movies only occasionally and selectively and who, like me, love the movies—sometimes in bafflement and exasperation—but love them.

For them, I hope *The Flicks*, along with evoking a few memories, will help explain where the movies were, why they left, where they are, and where they may be heading.

Foreword

by Alfred Hitchcock

Motion picture critics, mercifully do not ask that we love them. A goodly number, in fact, appear to find fulfillment of the most bizarre kind when the object of their carping and scolding turns upon them in the wake of an unfavorable review with nasty telephone calls, poison pen letters, demands to the publisher for instant dismissal, full-page advertisements designed to discredit and shame, and an occasional punch in the nose. Counter-attacks more often than not are the critic's meat and ale. Extra celebrity is to be gained by making capital of it—reprinting the howls of anguish, or describing how it feels to take a fist in the face or midriff; the more famous the infuriated one and the more overt his reaction to a bad review, the greater the accruing glory to the critic, the hotter the spotlight.

Now I have never known Charles Champlin to require love from those whose films he evaluates and I venture to say he would bristle with tempered outrage at the suggestion that he would even suffer it. Yet I am convinced that were there a fine instrument to measure waves of affection flowing from artist to critic (and what a wasteful contrivance that would be!), the nervous needle would show Champlin commanding more warmth of feeling from Hollywood's denizens than any of his colleagues coast-to-coast.

The special fondness for the man which exists in the film community (most people call him Chuck; I have never been able to bring myself to call so splendid a fellow by a name that is also a cut of beef, and far from the best at that) has nothing to do with his cherubic handsomeness and it does not follow that his kris is dull-edged. Far from it. The Arts Editor of the *Los Angeles Times*, whose functions extend beyond the business of merely reviewing films, can cut to the bone and draw blood with the best of them. But for the most part, he resists the cruel slash past the epidermis, holds spleen in tight check, and manages through a most adroit and felicitous manipulation of the English language to convey distaste and disappointment. One is not merely injured, one is reprimanded as a creative artist.

Why then the warm regard in which

Charles Champlin is held by producers, directors, screenwriters and actors alike (I can't speak for his readers)? I rather think it is for his graceful prose, devoid of that studied exhibitionistic tone to be found in much film criticism today; his willingness, always, to credit the high intentions of filmmakers, regardless of their failure to realize them; and for what seems to me to be a strong and unique sense of responsibility to the cinema form itself.

For my part, I have always found him to be eminently fair, though I have been nicked once or twice, and, with Richard Schickel and a very few others, to be the least terrifying of all critics. I might add that he also endears himself to me with his passion for suspense and mystery, and savors, as I do, those classic British murder cases that involve the most ordinary of people in the most extraordinary of circumstances. We have met in London, where he needs only a bowler hat and a bumbershoot to melt into the passing crowd; in Cannes, where he dutifully views a multitude of dreary films, risking permanent damage to eye, spine and brain; and in other places on his film festival rounds. Abroad, as well as on his home base, he strikes me as being the ideal motion picture critic in his refusal to become obsessively fixated on the cinema and in his exquisite detachment from those beguiling larger-than-life images. He regards motion pictures as the great dramatic medium of our time, but shares with me the realization that, after all, "It is only a movie," no reason to lose one's head and heart over it.

Whatever Became of Andy Hardy? is pure Champlin, no Mumbo Jumbo to it, none of the psychological balderdash that is the stock-in-trade of far too many chroniclers of the Hollywood scene. It is good to have him here in Our Town as a critic-essayist of the highest integrity and gratifying to know that his first book, long overdue, will win him new readers throughout the world.

*This book is dedicated to Mickey Rooney,
the principal citizen of that lost and
lovely world of Andy Hardy.*

Whatever became of Andy Hardy?

The prosperous, tree-shaded Middle-American world of Judge Hardy and his son Andrew seems now, in retrospect, to have been an almost perfect embodiment of the gifts Hollywood gave us in its Golden Age.

The Andy Hardy movies were certainly not the greatest to come out of the thirties, but they help define that Hollywood at its best. They were made by the most potent, efficient, and star-filled of all the great studios, Metro-Goldwyn-Mayer in Culver City, and they were crafted to that smooth and shining perfection that was MGM's hallmark. The fact that the first Hardy movie—a program picture for which no one at the studio seems to have held uncommon expectations—quickly became a series reflected an organization closely and cleverly attuned to its audience.

When *A Family Affair*, written by Kay Van Riper from a play called *Skidding* by Aurania Rouverol, was released in 1937, its principal attraction and the center of its plot was Lionel Barrymore as Judge Hardy. But what caught the eye of the customers and the theater men, as the sales department quickly reported back to Culver City, was the relationship between the judge and his son, played by the rising child star Mickey Rooney.

Miss Van Riper wrote another script, *You're Only Young Once*, with Lewis Stone taking over as Judge Hardy from Barrymore, who was unavailable, and with Fay Holden replacing Spring Byington as Mrs. Hardy. *Judge Hardy's Children* followed only four months later—the movies could really move in those days—and in 1938 the fourth in the series, *Love Finds Andy Hardy*, introduced Judy Garland as Andy's girl friend and became the most memorable and delightful of all the Hardy films. A newcomer named Lana Turner was also on hand, and so in the various films were Kathryn Grayson, Donna Reed, Ann Rutherford, and Esther Williams as well.

Carvel, Idaho, its last, disintegrating traces still barely recognizable on the MGM backlot as of the mid-1970s, depicted the world not

Mickey Rooney as Andy Hardy was funny but not usually as silly as he looked in this early publicity still, deerstalker hat, foliage, and all.

The Hardy family of Carvel: father (Lewis Stone), son (Mickey Rooney), aunt (Sara Haden), mother (Fay Holden), and Andy's older sister (Cecilia Parker). Lionel Barrymore was the first father.

as it was but as it ought to have been, with virtues intact, pieties unfeigned, commandments unbroken, good rewarded, evil foiled. There were problems and crises, but none that could not be tidily solved, usually by the generous application of good sense and fatherly advice, by the end of the last reel.

Swift, funny, folksy, touching, heart-warming, innocent, optimistic, positive, the Hardy movies were the apotheosis of the Hollywood version of the good American life: God-centered, orderly, advancing always toward every man's dream of comfort and security. Not surprisingly, as Bosley Crowther described in *Hollywood Rajah*, Louis B. Mayer took a close personal interest in the series and particularly in Andy as a model of the good son. When Rooney as Andy prayed for his mom to get well in *Judge Hardy and His Son*, the prayer had been dictated by Mayer himself

on bended knee and in tears, to the astonishment of the writer, Carey Wilson. The vision of the good life was also, and strongly, Mayer's.

In all, there were fourteen Hardy films before Mickey Rooney left to join the Army in 1943. After he was discharged in 1946, the studio eagerly began again, with *Love Laughs at Andy Hardy*, but by then it was too late—too late for Rooney to play Andy Hardy, but more important, too late for moviegoers to accept that special, dreamy vision of a serene and settled society. The movie died, and so did the Hollywood in which Andy Hardy had been born.

Andy Hardy is a figure from an attractive but irretrievably remote and different past. He has yielded to a drunken college professor snarling at his wife over their imaginary child, to a stud hustler from Texas trying to conquer Manhattan, to an American expatriate acting out his self-loathing in a shadowy Paris apartment with a girl whose name he does not know.

It is now clear that by the end of 1946 the Golden Age of Hollywood, Andy Hardy's Hollywood, had reached a historical peak of power, attendance, profitability, and persuasiveness—and had swiftly begun to change forever under the impact of several revolutionary forces, of which the greatest was and still is television.

What is astonishing is how fast it all happened and how predictable it all was (or should have been). Almost overnight, the role of the movies in society was permanently shifted, and with the shift commenced a fundamental change in the nature of the movies, an evolution whose ultimate consequences cannot be predicted even now. Time and television have changed permanently the look of the industry and the look of the movies. From being *the* mass medium of entertainment, the motion picture—although still a mass and massive medium—became the minority medium, displaced by television, a new art form that, like the motion picture, exists in an uneasy and inexact tension between art and commerce.

Now, more than thirty years later, the relationships between the theatrical motion picture and television continue to change. After truculent beginnings Hollywood, both as a specific place and as a symbol of the film industry, has learned to accommodate and prosper from television as well as cinema, although there are many convincing signs that the major studios will never again be major in the ways they were in pretelevision times.

Here shy sweethearts in Love Finds Andy Hardy, *Mickey and Judy did nine more films together.*

Producing series or movies for television is as hazardous to fiscal health as making theatrical films. While Hollywood's total output is probably as high as it has ever been, and possibly even higher, the miles of film and tape have not brought back the expansive stability of the prosperous past.

The abiding irony is that the movies have lost their majority, their assured and automatic audiences, and their confidence, but they have gained their maturity. During a quarter-century or more of economic chaos and precipitously declining attendance, incessant changes in corporate ownership and management, and agonizing readjustments in work styles, the movies have come of age as a creative form. They have won (if they have not

5

always made the most of) a freedom of expression unsurpassed in either the novel or the drama. If the movies are fewer than ever, the best of them are very arguably better than ever, combining an ever-advancing technical mastery with an almost totally unfettered ability to reflect life as it really is.

In the early years of television, it appeared obvious that survival for the theatrical motion picture surely lay in doing what television could not do as well, or could not do at all. The urgent logic of that truth was the principal, if not the only, force behind the opening up of the screen.

But nothing in the equation between movies and television is constant except change and, as in many other areas of life, the rate of change is accelerating. The movies used their new-won freedom to best advantage in the pursuit of social realism, as in the portrayals of urban half-life in *Midnight Cowboy* and *Panic in Needle Park,* or in the projection of a harrowing near-future in *A Clockwork Orange.* The movies continue to be so various that generalizations are risky, but it is obvious that the flirtation with hard reality, which fell upon hard times at the box office, is now over or has been set aside indefinitely. *One Flew Over the Cuckoo's Nest,* the finest picture of 1976, was the exception that proved the general surrender of the movies to "pure" escapist stuff in one form or another. Once again and more emphatically than ever, the Hollywood wisdom is that for their survival the movies must out-star, out-spectacle, out-sex, and out-violence television.

The vigorous successes of *Airport* in 1969 and *The Poseidon Adventure* in 1972, among other splashy works, set off a bandwagon dash into starry, gaudy, and expensive films that translated disasters of every kind, man-made and natural, into entertainment. The extraordinary commercial triumph of *Jaws* in 1976 seemed to confirm and reconfirm the Holly-

Founded in Brooklyn in 1899, Vitagraph came west to these splendid Hollywood studios, now the site of a television station, in 1916. Later the company merged with Warner Brothers.

wood wisdom about where the audience is and what it wants. The spend-money-to-make-money formula does not invariably pay off, and such big-starred and large-budget movies as *Hindenburg* and *Lucky Lady* failed. But the successes have come frequently enough to keep the bandwagon rolling. The

danger for those who love the movies is that the infatuation with scale leads to a narrowing of the kinds of movies that get made. The new and unsurpassed freedom of expression too often finds little or nothing worth saying.

The irony is that television is now able to spike its bland family entertainment with occasional dramas of substance, enjoying a new boldness and freedom of its own. It addresses themes—homosexuality (in *That Certain Summer*), euthanasia, rape, venereal disease—that would have been impossible or cruelly difficult for the movies themselves to touch as recently as a decade ago. In *The Migrants*, with its uncompromising look at the exploitation of farm labor, and *The Autobiography of Miss Jane Pittman*, a harsh chronicling of a century of racial prejudice, television has presented social issues that modern-day moviemakers would have been hard-pressed to get financed. Yet neither form has touched its limits. After more than a quarter of a century, television and the movies continue to evoke changes in each other.

A comedy factory, Mack Sennett's studio arose in Edendale just east of Hollywood.

The founding movie moguls are gone—the Mayers, Warners, Cohns, Disneys—replaced by moviemakers whose names are largely unknown outside the industry, though it probably doesn't matter much one way or the other because the men and women themselves are apt to be gone in a month, season, or year.

Half of the MGM backlot has been sold off to real estate developers and is filled with condominiums while the rest of the land awaits a buyer. The sound stages of the old Columbia studio on Gower Street in Holly-wood are now rental tennis courts, a temporary usage until someone buys the whole property. Columbia now shares with Warner Brothers the Burbank lot that Jack Warner and his brothers built, and the savings in overhead are worth several million dollars a year to each studio. Most of the original Twentieth Century-Fox backlot south of Pico Boulevard has given way to a shining-tower com-

Universal's first landmark, a water tank, dominated some doomed San Fernando Valley farmland, where the studio opened in 1915.

plex of apartment-office buildings and a shopping-entertainment center appropriately called Century City, and the days of all that is left are numbered. Charlie Chaplin's studio on La Brea Avenue is now headquarters for Herb Alpert's Tijuana Brass and their A&M Records. Disney prospers, though only half its revenues and its profits are from movies, the rest from Disneyland and Disney World. Only Universal still retains the bustling big studio aura of the older Hollywood, complete with a fully articulated power structure. The

studio's sleek twin black office towers, rising on the site of the chicken ranch Uncle Carl Laemmle bought in 1915, evoke new times and old, and the corporation that gave us Ma and Pa Kettle is now the biggest and most profitable purveyor of television fare. It found the secret of film success with *The Sting* and, perhaps most significantly, capitalizes on the

9

continuing lure of Hollywood by attracting thousands of paying customers daily year-round to its spectacular studio tours.

In bad times and in better the movies have remained a source of unparalleled fascination for a worldwide public. Not the least of the ironies surrounding Hollywood and the movies is that even as attendance was plunging by the tens of millions, a new generation was confidently proclaiming that the motion picture is the art form of these decades, if not indeed of this whole century. Film has become the language of children as words were the language of their parents. Inexpensive Super-8 cameras have made filmmaking as possible and provocative for the young creator as writing the Great American Novel was for his grandfather.

For all of us who love film, but perhaps most keenly for the young, the movies have a special dynamism, the sense of being a territory still only partially discovered, and some of whose earliest explorers—Frank Capra, Allan Dwan, Jean Renoir, Alfred Hitchcock, Luis Buñuel, King Vidor—are alive and among us. Just this sense of inexhaustible possibility, of capacities for both strength and subtlety not yet found, draws us to the movies and, a little less hopefully, to television.

The essential function of the movies has not changed. Their aim is still to engross us, to make the screen dissolve and the camera disappear, and to thrust us into the consciousnesses of people who are not ourselves. And the principal allure of the movies has not changed either. We go to the flicks primarily to be entertained, distracted, to find escape from what is humdrum, confining, discouraging, and unpleasant in our ordinary lives.

But whatever *did* become of Andy Hardy? While we may feel wistful about his world with its certitudes and its tidy, happy resolutions, it is long gone and not to be recaptured, even in the name of pure entertainment.

The end of the line, Andy Hardy Comes Home, *was made by MGM for television in 1958, and had Rooney's own son, Teddy, playing a new Hardy generation, but the film did poorly.*

It is not simply that the movies have changed. We have changed and the world has changed: they don't make movies the way they used to because the world isn't the way it used to be. The movies have changed drastically principally because the nature and expectations of the audience are so sharply different, so much more sophisticated and more demanding, than they once were. An audience saturated by thirty years of television may no longer be quite sure what it likes, but it knows what is bad. Our collective conclusions about what is entertaining are broader than they were. Audiences want no one kind of movie as a steady diet, but increasingly demand excellence equally from the Disney comedy as well as the Bergman tragedy.

A world-embracing diversity has always been central to the movies' charm and power. The distinction between now and then is that the diversity exists in depth as well as in breadth. There are the romps and the shallow frolics, but there are also the explorations of deep space and the dark, strangled soul.

The years since 1946 have been nothing less than revolutionary. The span is from the golden peak of the movies-as-commerce to the black depths of despair of the movies-as-endangered-species, the obituaries prematurely prepared. In taking a critic's-eye look at film's long fight back and at the birth and swift maturing of television as the medium that changed the movies and all our lives, we arrive at the murmuring edge of yet a further revolution, of cables and cassettes and what they may portend for the beleaguered Bijou. Nowadays the movies seem to be their own best suspense story.

Like most suspense stories, Hollywood's time of troubles began amidst a deceptive calm, a calm you would have said was only logical after the storms of war ended in 1945.

11

The end of the beginnings

Measured along the larger sweeps of history, the movies are even now very young. It is just eighty years since they were first projected for profit in the middle of the 1890s, which means there are men still living who are older than the movies. Adolph Zukor, who founded Paramount Pictures in its modern corporate form and who was honored at a large Hollywood banquet on his hundredth birthday in 1973, was already in his twenties when the movies began. (By the time he died in 1976, Zukor's extraordinary lifetime had also encompassed the birth of electricity, powered flight, radio, television, and rockets to the moon and Mars.)

Though the movies are chronologically young, they developed very rapidly, like almost everything else in the twentieth century. By 1910 there were already more than 10,000 movie theaters in the United States, many of them converted stores, located near and playing primarily to working-class audiences. The new films were a novelty, and had more in common with vaudeville and the penny arcades than with the theater. From the start movies would not stay defined or be limited.

The creative possibilities of the movies expanded to accommodate the genius of the men and women who worked in them, and it was the movies' stroke of uncanny good luck that a sometime actor named David Wark Griffith called on Biograph Studios in New York hoping to sell some story lines. He was pressed into service as a director, and he proved to have an intuitive gift for telling stories in the motion-picture form. If he did not invent it (and in many specifics he did), he demonstrated the whole vocabulary of movie language as it exists today, from the close-up to the tracking shot to cross-cutting and fade-outs.

Almost single-handedly Griffith led the movies out of their primitive beginnings, when they were one-reelers, essentially skits photographed from a fixed camera position. Griffith increased the complexity of the nar-

Theda Bara as Cleopatra, *first filmed by Fox in 1917, summed up the exotic, steamy, and dreamy extravagance of the romantic silents.*

rative lines, developed a stock company of star players including Mary Pickford, the Gish sisters, and Donald Crisp, and stretched the running times from two reels to four and five and in 1915 to the twelve reels of *The Birth of a Nation*, the first authentic full-length masterpiece of the movies. It has a technical brilliance still unsurpassed, still breathtaking.

Even as Griffith was learning his trade (or inventing it) in the very early 1900s, the economic basis of the motion-picture industry—renting prints instead of selling them outright—was also beginning to take shape. The explosive popularity of the movies and the insatiable demand for more product, which made renting more prudent than buying—or selling—prints outright, took the movies from something like a cottage craft to a uniquely colorful industry in a very short time. As *The Birth of a Nation* was being released in 1915, Carl Laemmle was establishing his Universal Pictures in the San Fernando Valley.

A founding generation of filmmakers and entrepreneurs led by Griffith himself, Jesse Lasky, Sam Goldwyn, Laemmle, the Brothers Warner and the Brothers Cohn and the Brothers Disney, Louis B. Mayer and William Fox and dozens of others less talented or less lucky, planted themselves and their works in the steady Southern California sunlight.

By 1926 there were 20,000 movie houses across the United States and the glory that was Hollywood was in full blossom. Harold Lloyd was said to earn $40,000 a week, Charlie Chaplin $30,000, Douglas Fairbanks, Sr. $24,000. The major studios were becoming mammoth self-contained enterprises, from their anonymous writers to their theaters, many of which were so elaborate they could have been sets for *Scheherazade*. The lives of the Hollywood great were followed in detail in households around the world in which the names of William Shakespeare, Karl Marx, and even Edgar A. Guest were unknown.

The master at work, David Wark Griffith, with megaphone in hand, directs Intolerance *in 1916 as Billy Bitzer cranks the camera and child actor Ben Alexander looks on.*

The first movie masterpiece (overleaf) *Griffith's* Birth of a Nation *in 1915, gave epic scale to a Confederate retreat.*

Radio posed a brief threat, which the coming of talking pictures defeated. By 1930 the movies all sang, all danced, all talked, and nearly 90 million Americans listened and watched each week (a peak of attendance not to be exceeded until 1946). The year 1930 may have marked the end of the first era of American film, its age of both gaudy and maverick innocence.

Later legend says the movies were depression-proof, but this is only relatively true. Attendance and revenues slumped throughout the thirties. Nevertheless, Louis B. Mayer remained the highest-paid executive in the country during those years. Despite the economic uncertainties, the studio system settled into its finest hours. Most of Hollywood's notable stars, from Cagney to Gable to Garland, made their appearances and their reputations. The great Hollywood directors—King Vidor, Raoul Walsh, Howard Hawks, Frank Capra, John Ford, Michael Curtiz, William Wyler, George Cukor, William Wellman, George Stevens, and all the others—did some of their most impressive work. The great majority of the more than 6,000 pre-1948 Hollywood films—which now keep the used-car commercials from bumping head on in the middle of the night—came from the great decade of the 1930s.

Then, in 1946, American movies hit what proved to be their historical peak of attendance, profitability, and power. They had lost most of their rich foreign markets, which had come to constitute a third or more of their total business. But at home they had been just about the only entertainment game in town, the principal public pleasure a wartime gas-rationed country could get to; and they had prospered.

Estimates vary widely, but a reasonable calculation is that in 1946 the movies in the United States drew an average of 90 million customers each week. The Department of

A triumph of the golden years, Jimmy Cagney's Yankee Doodle Dandy (1942) won him an Oscar.

Commerce figure on the total box-office receipts for that year is a shade under $1.7 billion. The number of films produced in Hollywood had dropped from 546 in 1942 to 425 in 1946, but the net film rentals received by Hollywood, so *Fortune* magazine figured, had increased from $300 million to $400 million in the same years.

Moviegoing was, as it had always been, a national habit. The 90 million admissions

were heavy with repeaters, because we all went to the movies, instead of to a movie. Yet lately there had been a difference: the habit had been sustained by the circumstances of wartime. There had been hints in the late prewar years that the composition of the audience was changing—surveys showed that a relatively small, young fraction of the population constituted a fairly large percentage of the total admissions.

What seemed to be a peak was in fact an end. Hollywood's luck turned bad overnight, and the timing could not have been worse.

If the movies were still young, the industry was middle-aged and beyond. It had been largely the creation of a single generation, the founding moguls who were themselves at middle age or past it. They had grown rich and often autocratic, but their positions proved in some instances to be surprisingly insecure; and they were frequently caught up in the power struggles of corporations that had come to be sharply divided between the creative community on the West Coast and the financial forces on the East Coast. Louis B. Mayer was an early and most conspicuous casualty,

forced in 1951 to resign from the studio he had done the most to build and that bore his name.

What mattered was that at a time when deep-seated social changes were affecting the movies and calling for imaginative and flexible leadership, Hollywood was caught up in the problem of shifting its controls to another generation, a maneuver for which it was evidently totally unprepared and for which it had little enthusiasm.

The revolutionary changes confronting the movies were, in approximately chronological order, the implications of the end of World War II, the dawn of commercial television, the loss of the studios' theater chains through antitrust decree, and, far from least, a crisis over what the motion picture ought to be, what it should say and to whom—the crisis of Andy Hardy's future.

The war-delayed aspirations hit first: Americans began moving to new places and into new homes, returning to their studies, traveling and camping and renewing their interest in sports. The movies, which had gotten nearly ninety cents of every amusement dollar spent in wartime, began to have less of it. By 1969, they were receiving only forty-eight cents of the amusement dollar.

The postwar residential flight to the suburbs transformed midtown picture palaces into triple-feature grind-houses or skin-flick centers, if they survived at all, and many didn't.

The antitrust action against Hollywood had actually begun before the war. In 1938 the Department of Justice filed a 119-page complaint charging Paramount, Loew's, Inc. (the parent firm of MGM), and the six other major studios with violations of the Sherman Antitrust Act, specifically with monopolistic practices in the making, distributing, and showing of motion pictures. The underlying issue was the practice of block-booking, under which an

independent theater had to contract to take a studio's package of films, sight unseen, for a given period. The independent theaters thus had almost no bargaining power and no choice, and sought relief. The whole question was pushed aside by the war; then in 1948 the Supreme Court ruled that the practice of block-booking was in fact in restraint of trade.

Between 1950 and 1954, the "big five" studios that owned theaters—Paramount, RKO, Fox, Warner's, MGM—all entered into consent decrees with the Justice Department to sell off their theater holdings. It hurt because these studios, which had previously been assured of at least some revenue from each of their pictures, no matter how awful they were, faced a diminishing audience once they had no captive theaters of their own.

The major crisis was, naturally, posed by the rampaging young giant, television, whose appearance and enormous acceptance appears to have caught Hollywood unawares (see Chapter 3). The studios' first responses were defensive: the new medium would go away, and Hollywood would help it go away by refusing to sell it any of its older films. But when the Bank of America, which had been stuck with a vaultful of films as the result of a foreclosure action, sold them to television, the rush to sell was on.

Not until 1951, when television had been around for five years, did one of the majors decide to join rather than fight. In that year Columbia established a television arm, Screen Gems, a decision that later kept the whole studio afloat during a stretch of catastrophic theatrical releases. Screen Gems, marketing the Columbia film library and also producing for television, turned profits from the start.

In the end, all the other crises afflicting the movies came to bear on what the industry crisply calls "the product." It seems clear now that increasingly over the years a gap had opened between life as it was lived and life

Hollywood goes to war and produces inspirational favorite, Greer Garson and Walter Pidgeon braving the bombs in Mrs. Miniver *in 1942.*

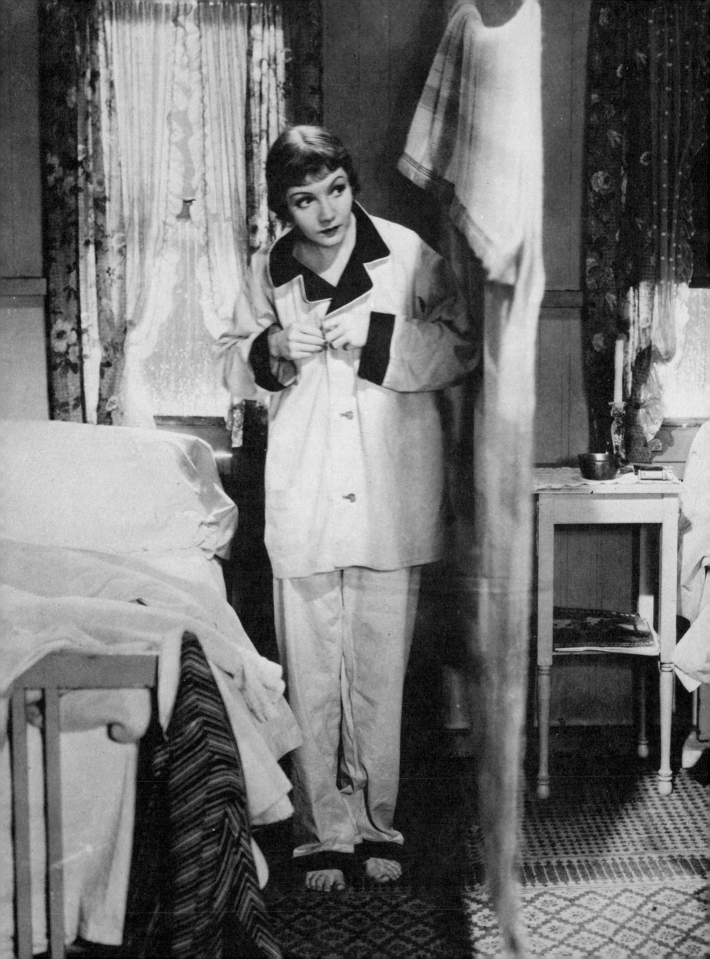

as it was reflected in Hollywood's movies. The effect of the Hays Code from the early 1930s had been to overprotect us, to impose a vision of life that was harder and harder to square with the realities around us. It is not without interest that the Kinsey report on *Sexual Behavior in the Human Male*, chronicling the gradual changes in American mores over the previous quarter-century, was published in 1948, when under the Code as both written and interpreted it was still impossible to show a married couple occupying a double bed.

While no single event caused American moviemakers—and their audiences—to rebel against the Code's proscriptions and Hollywood's outmoded brand of morality, a handful of neorealistic postwar Italian films made a profound impression throughout the film world. The harsh vitality and gritty credibility of these now-classic films (discussed in Chapter 4) carried the seeds of a creative revolution in attitudes toward filmmaking.

What had been the best of times suddenly became the worst of times. Production shrank from 425 films in 1946 to 405 in 1948, slipped further to 354 in 1953, and to fewer than 300 in 1954. Those 90 million admissions a week in 1946 had dropped to 46 million in 1954, on their way to a low of around 17 million tickets a week at the start of the 1970s.

A Hollywood joke of the fifties acknowledged the tough times. A film executive's tot was said to have turned in a school essay that said, "Mommy is poor, Daddy is poor, even the servants are poor." And indeed it was not yet breadline time. There were reserves, and revenues from motion-picture sales to dreaded television. And the industry remained convinced that there were ways to fight back, offerings the customer simply could not refuse. The movie moguls were not wrong, but it took a painful while to discover where the future lay.

Daring then, charming still, Frank Capra's classic It Happened One Night *kept Claudette Colbert and Clark Gable pure with a thin blanket.*

Ready, sets, go!

The wonder is that television took Hollywood by such baleful surprise. The medium had not, after all, appeared overnight, as if by magic. Its technological footings went back to the nineteenth century, and television as such had been working—experimentally, crudely, but working—since the 1920s. The medium was a long time aborning. Only an industry as obsessed with itself, as savagely competitive within itself, and as self-satisfied and insulated from much other reality as Hollywood, could have ignored so successfully, and then underestimated so drastically, the invention that spelled revolutionary change and trouble for the dreammakers.

The idea of television, like the idea of flight, had been around for a long time before anyone knew how to make it happen. A German named Paul Nipkow had invented, in 1884, a scanning device that made it possible to transmit still pictures by wire. The principle of the scanner—breaking down images into pieces of information—is what makes televi-

sion work, and after those early experiments it was only a matter of time until television took over our lives.

An American, C. F. Jenkins, came up with an improved scanner in 1925. In England, John Baird was granted an experimental television license in 1926. H. E. Ives of American Telephone & Telegraph transmitted a picture of President Herbert Hoover from New York to Washington in 1927. The National Broadcasting Company began experimental television broadcasting over its station W2XBS in New York. AT&T made experimental transmissions in *color* that same year. The first full-length feature film to be broadcast on television was *The Crooked Tree* (starring Ben Lyon, Zasu Pitts, and James Gleason), which was shown on Los Angeles station W6XAO (now KHJ-TV) on March 10, 1933. But the movie industry at that time was far more concerned about the growth of radio, which hastened the end of silent films. The introduction of talking pictures doubled the

An early television favorite, Tennessee Ernie Ford, here used the medium's trick-shot technology for a musical number on his show.

movie audience between 1927 and 1929: who could care about television?

The British Broadcasting Corporation began experimental transmissions in London in 1929, using a crude 30-line system; and in 1936, the BBC began regular daily television broadcasting, having adopted a system developed by Electrical Musical Industries (EMI) that provided 415-line pictures. Also in 1936, German television broadcast the Berlin Olympics to an estimated 50,000 viewers. The next year, the BBC broadcast the coronation of King George VI and reached an audience also estimated at 50,000 viewers, in and around London.

Television's day was drawing closer, but so was the outbreak of World War II. The American public did not get its first real look at television until the New York World's Fair in 1939, when Radio Corporation of America demonstrated its 441-line system to tens of thousands of fascinated fairgoers. Between 1930 and 1939 the company had spent $9 million on television by a team under the leadership of Vladimir Zworykin.

(One of American television's earliest watchers was the distinguished essayist E. B. White. In his "One Man's Meat" column in *Harper's* magazine in June 1938, White wrote, "I believe television is going to be the test of the modern world, and that in this new opportunity to see beyond the range of our vision we shall discover either a new and unbearable disturbance of the general peace or a saving radiance in the sky. We shall stand or fall by television—of that I am quite sure. . . . When I was a child people simply looked about them and were moderately happy; today they peer beyond the seven seas, bury themselves waist deep in tidings, and by and large what they see and hear makes them unutterably sad.")

In 1941 RCA's experimental station was licensed in New York for commercial broad-

Invading enemy territory in the 1940s, television had an early outpost in RCA's Hollywood offices near Sunset and Vine.

casting as WNBT. On the same day, the Columbia Broadcasting System received a commercial license for its experimental station, W2XAB (now WCBS), also in New York. Commercial telecasting was poised to begin. But the outbreak of war had already forced the closing down of BBC television for the duration, and the entry of America into the war after Pearl Harbor effectively stopped television in its tracks. As the war began, there were six licensed stations and perhaps 10,000 receivers in the United States.

The speed with which television grew, once the war was finally over in 1945, is even now

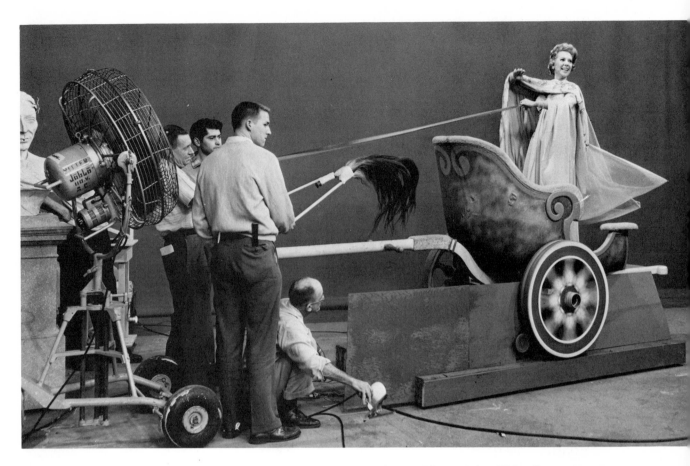

Charioteer Dinah Shore was drawn by a horseless tail on her Chevy Show, which was admired for its imaginative stagings.

staggering to contemplate. At the beginning of 1948 there were seventeen stations in eight cities; by the end of 1948 there were forty-three stations in twenty-three cities, and the audience had multiplied in that year alone by 4,000 percent. Those were the days when there were probably as many sets in saloons as in living rooms, when the cabinets were large and the screens small, and when watching kinescopes of "Broadway Open House" (Dagmar and Morey Amsterdam) was like looking at the action through pieces of wet toast. The hours, as in radio, were still divided into fifteen-minute segments; one fifteen-

minute show, "Hair-raising Tales," was essentially a bizarre quarter-hour hair-oil commercial, but it was watched, like everything else, with awed attention.

"Uncle Miltie" Berle became television's first major personality with his "Texaco Star Theater," and Ed Sullivan in 1948 was commencing his even longer tenure with "Toast of the Town," the variety show later renamed for its solemn host. Also broadcast in 1948: the Metropolitan Opera's *Otello*, suggesting one facet of television's incalculable cultural influence.

Television's coverage of the 1948 national political conventions was convincingly prophetic of the enormous impact the medium would be having in the area of news and public affairs. (With a nice irony, NBC's coverage of the conventions was co-sponsored and also largely staffed by *Life* magazine, which would eventually be driven out of business by television.)

By 1948 there were 250,000 sets in use; a year later, a million. In 1951 televisions outsold radios for the first time, and by 1952, 15 million television sets were in use. With the coaxial cable and microwave relays linking the ends of the nation, television could reach 60 percent of American homes.

The consequences of all this for the movies were, of course, merely colossal. They were terrific for Hollywood in the pure sense of inspiring terror, although the new medium also inspired some catastrophically misjudged contempt. RCA's General David Sarnoff came West personally to offer Louis B. Mayer a big share of NBC in the hopes of making MGM a producing partner in the network. If accepted, the offer would have rewritten the later history of the studio and of Mayer himself. Mayer not only turned it down but also forbade his employees to watch television. One story was that simply using the word "television" in the halls of the Thalberg Building at MGM was ground for instant firing. From the fat profits of the wartime years, Metro went into sharp reverse and operated in 1947–48 at a $6.5 million loss. In mid-1952 Dore Schary, then in charge of production at the studio, announced pay cuts for all 4,000 MGM employees. After a couple of seasons of narrow profit, Metro was in the red again, $3 million worth, for the 1955–56 year.

It was much the same elsewhere in Hollywood. In early 1953, Warner Brothers announced pay cuts of up to 50 percent for its employees, and the studio shut down for ninety days. The brothers themselves, Jack and Harry, had been on the verge of selling out in disgust and retiring two years earlier, but the deal, with a syndicate including Bulova Watch, had fallen through.

A new day for sports, symbolized by 1948 World Series telecast, came with the medium's huge home audiences and commercial revenues, which now keep many professional teams alive.

By one estimate, movie-theater attendance dropped by more than half in the decade between 1946 and 1956. By another estimate, one-fourth of the 19,000 theaters in the United States closed between 1946 and 1953. Fascinated by the blue glow in the living room, the audience was staying home. A bitter Hollywood joke of the period involved the man who called his neighborhood theater to find out what time the show started. "What time can you get here?" the manager asked.

Hollywood dropped its stars, cut its costs, made fewer films, and aimed for spectacle. The industry tried 3D, with *House of Wax* in 1953, and changed the dimensions of the screen with Cinerama, Cinemascope, Vista Vision, and Todd-AO. The fall in total attendance went on.

Meantime, the new medium skated between fatuity and triumph. The roller derby hit TV early, in 1948, but there was also the genial ethnicity of "The Goldbergs" and the easy urbane charm of Dave Garroway in the popular "Garroway at Large" from Chicago. Late in 1950 the first television soap opera appeared—"The First 100 Years."

In the fall of 1950 and the spring of 1951 there were the televised hearings of Senator Estes Kefauver's subcommittee to investigate interstate crime in America. Some 20 million Americans watched every day and made temporary stars of the slow-voiced senator himself; his colleague, Senator Charles Tobey, with his chirpy New England outrage ("These vermin!" he cried); and Rudolph Halley, the committee's chief inquisitor. The immediacy and the drama of these televised hearings—the cameras focused on Frank Costello's hands, avoiding the gangster's face to safeguard his life—were powerful stuff. And anyone who watched will never forget the late Senator Joseph R. McCarthy droning "Mr. Chairman, Mr. Chairman . . . point of order!" during the televised Army-McCarthy hearings in

Television's first early morning stars were Host Dave Garroway and his chimp pals J. Fred Muggs and Phoebe B. Beebe of the Today *show, an innovative program idea.*

The new medium's persuasive power was hugely proved by Edward R. Murrow's dramatic attack on Senator Joseph McCarthy on See It Now, *after which McCarthy's influence fell.*

1954. Like the Kefauver hearings, this live drama brought all activity to a stand still while it was being shown, as the Watergate hearings were to do two decades later.

In an attempt, late even then, to impose order on the chaotic and explosive growth of television, the Federal Communications Commission had in the late 1940s put a tem-

The Great Caesar—Sid—a master of slapstick, sight gags and verbal humor, led a comedy team that made Your Show of Shows *one of early television's brightest hours.*

porary freeze on new licenses. Then in April 1952 the FCC issued its *Sixth Report and Order.* Among other things, it set the television dial as it still is, with a dozen Very High Frequency channels—number 2 through number 13—and seventy Ultra High Frequency channels, numbers 14 through 83. It also set aside 10 percent of future licenses for noncommercial, educational stations. It was a nice gesture; the catch was that in sixty-nine of the top one hundred markets there was no VHF channel assigned to educational television: none, for example, in New York, Philadelphia, Cleveland, Washington, and Los Angeles, at least at that time. Public television, stuck largely with UHF channels, which are hard to receive in the best of conditions, was thus assured a minor and difficult second-class status within the whole spectrum of television. This has effectively left the medium at the mercy of marketplace ethics, advertiser control, and also lowest-common-denominator attitudes.

That public television has in fact been able to develop (or import) the programs it has and to command the audiences it has—and indeed to serve as the artistic conscience for all of television, as it does—is a tribute to the dedicated men and women who staff it and to the few foundations and major corporations that underwrite it, along with the millions of viewers who contribute financial support. The effective survival of public television owes almost nothing to government policy, which left to noncommercial uses essentially what commercial interests didn't want.

Indeed, in the early 1950s the growth of noncommercial broadcasting was yet to come, and series like "The Forsyte Saga" and "Sesame Street" had yet to give it the beginnings of a broad base of support.

Commercial television, on the other hand, continued to grow at an extraordinary rate. The competition between RCA and CBS over their respective color systems was resolved in 1953 in favor of the RCA system, which thus became the standard for the country. The first very modest sales of color sets (about 5,000 of them) began the following year, but the problems of gearing up for full-scale color transmission and production took another decade.

The soap opera, a staple of radio, switched easily to television, as in this mid-60s drama. The soaps, which have their own fan magazines, are watched by 20 million daily.

As staggering as the growth of television in its first decade had been—and by 1956 there were sets in some 37 million U.S. households—there was even more prodigious growth just ahead. It does not seem impossible to have predicted that television would reach such size and importance, nor indeed to have guessed that most of its production would come to be centered in Hollywood. But in television's first years, Hollywood for the most part seemed unsure whether it would go away, or whether it should be fought or could be fought, or whether it might doom the town no matter what anybody did.

But foresight was what movie moguls were made of, and one of them at least, the redoubtable Sam Goldwyn, writing in the New York *Times* (see chapter 5), found grounds for optimism in the challenge.

Arrivederci, Hollywood

The subtlest but not the least important of the revolutionary influences on American movies in the postwar period was their inoculation by the foreign strain.

Before World War II there had been almost no distribution of foreign-language films outside New York and a handful of other large cities. Even the campuses had not yet become congregations of film buffs. In the small town in upstate New York where I grew up, such foreign films as came along had snakes and lions and were made by Frank Buck or Martin and Osa Johnson. The first film I have any memory of was in fact a patronizing documentary about Africa in which a squatting native lit a whole box of kitchen matches, one after another. It went on interminably, and I asked to be taken home.

British movies were a bit more widely shown, but I doubt if I saw a half-dozen before I went off to Boston and college and met the rest of the world. The United States imported the filmmakers instead of the films —Alfred Hitchcock, Erich von Stroheim, Ernst Lubitsch, William Dieterle, Sergei Eisenstein (unsuccessfully), Fritz Lang, Jean Renoir, and all the others who did battle, usually painful, with an unyielding studio system.

With the probable exception of Hitchcock, who is still working and free to make the kind of movies he likes and does best (*Topaz* was an exception, an uncomfortable studio assignment), most of the foreign directors reached uneasy compromises with Hollywood, scaled from disastrous (von Stroheim) to wastefully disappointing (Renoir). ("He'll never be one of us," Darryl Zanuck is reported to have said, dismissing the idea of using Renoir again.)

However ill- or under-used they were, each of the directors left his mark on American filmmaking. Each influenced other filmmakers—Lubitsch with his elegant comedy, Lang with his emotional wattages and his feeling for the dark violence in the soul, Renoir with his understanding of the common humanity of us all. Each created an expanded awareness

The new film realism out of postwar Italy, first seen in Roberto Rosselini's Open City, *was to leave its mark on Hollywood.*

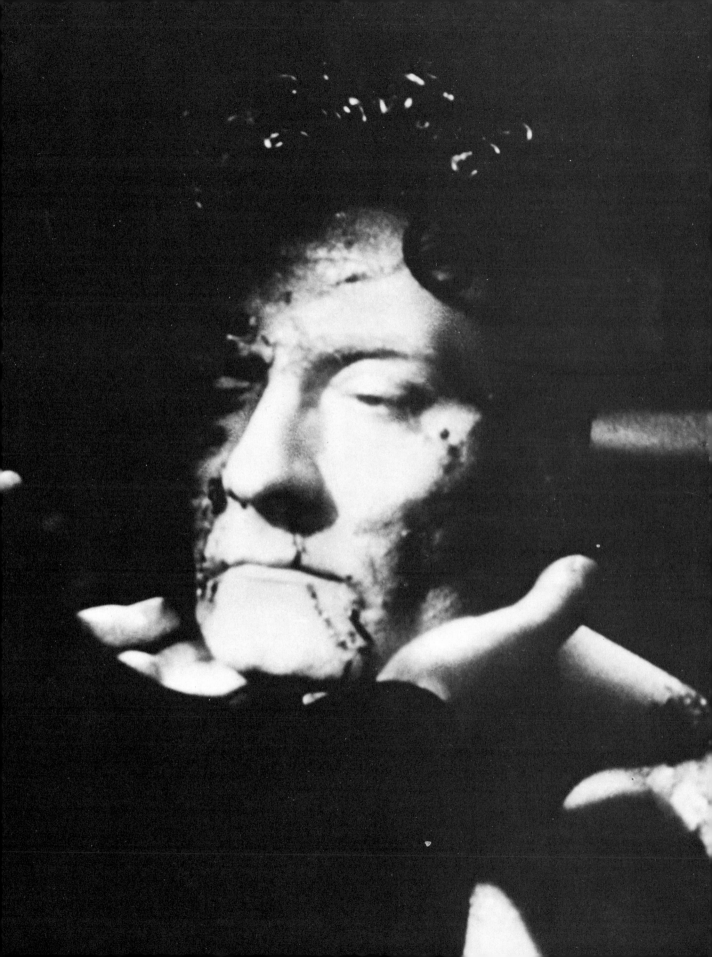

Sleek story-telling, embroiling Margaret Lockwood and Michael Redgrave in Alfred Hitchcock's The Lady Vanishes, *brightened prewar movies.*

of what the movies could do. But each, once in Hollywood, was reduced to testing the sharp limits of the conventional, commercial Hollywood wisdom.

The first postwar films, arriving from another continent, might have come from another world. And the first of these was Roberto Rossellini's *Open City* in 1945. No one who saw it in its initial release here is likely to forget the staggering impact it had. Written during the German occupation of Rome, it deals with a Gestapo sweep against the Italian

underground, particularly a priest, a widow, the man she is to marry and his friend, both Communists.

Rossellini shot the film on little money (so little that he could not afford to process the footage until he raised additional funds after the production was finished). He had even sold some of his clothes and furniture to keep

production going. He used actual locations almost entirely, because he could not afford to rent studio space. Some of the raw stock he scrounged in short lengths from the black market. He had no lights, and the film shows it. But the results, by both accident and intention, have the brusque, harsh, gray look of a news documentary investigating a violent and tragic story with the bitter reality of life itself amid the final convulsions of the war.

One of the Communists is executed. The Germans coldly gun down the widow (in sight

Harsh reality, unsentimental and uncompromised, as reflected here in Anna Magnani's anguish in Open City, *led all film a new way.*

of her young son) as she runs screaming after the truck carrying her man away. The priest is tortured and then—in one of the most brutal scenes in all of cinema—executed in public, again with the widow's son looking on through a fence.

Rossellini used street people in some roles and cast against type in others, persuading

Aldo Fabrizi, a music-hall comic, to play the tragic priest and Anna Magnani, herself a music-hall comedienne, to play the tragic working-class widow.

With *Open City* Rossellini had destroyed the polite perfections of filmmaking, denied the filmgoers' acceptance of make-believe, revoked the notion that an ultimate justice must always be seen to be operative. *Open City* was raw, immediate, unsparing, inescapable, shattering. It had its first screening in Rome in September 1945. The audience booed, probably because so many wartime passions and enmities still rankled, but it became the largest box-office attraction of the year in Italy.

It launched the astonishing decade of Italian neorealist films, so named by a critic because their "new" realism broke with romantic film conventions of the past. In the United States (and indeed around the world), *Open City* signaled the start of a revolution of rising expectations, among filmmakers and filmgoers alike, for the movies and what they might say or show about real life.

Joseph R. Levine, later known as the producer of *The Graduate* but then a regional distributor who handled *Open City* for the late Joseph Burstyn, calculated not long ago that the film probably played only 300 theaters in the United States in its initial release. A foreign film of comparable quality now could, Levine has estimated, hope for as many as 3,000 play dates. With *Open City*, the postwar invasion was just beginning.

It was followed the next year by Vittorio De Sica's *Shoeshine*, in which the postwar experience was lived through two young shoeshine boys, best friends, who are drawn into the amoral adult criminal world and toward tragedy in which one of the boys kills the other. More controlled and impressionistic than *Open City*, it was equally moving and won huge acclaim, including a special Oscar

Another masterpiece out of early postwar Italy, Vittorio De Sica's deeply moving film, Shoeshine, followed the fates of two street boys caught in the machineries of a brutally indifferent society.

in 1947 from the Motion Picture Academy (which had not yet started its awards for Best Foreign Language Film).

There were more stunning works to come: Rossellini's *Paisan* and *Germany Year Zero,* the brief, horrifying chronicle of a thirteen-year-old boy alone in the rubble of Berlin; De Sica's *The Bicycle Thief,* about a father and son trying to survive in the poverty of the postwar era; and *Umberto D,* the daily life of an elderly man in a society that has no place and no use for its aged. Like Rossellini, De Sica cast nonactors to heighten the credibility and the impact of his films. Umberto D was portrayed by a university professor. *The Bicycle Thief* won another special Oscar for De Sica in 1949.

By 1950 De Sica was doing *Miracle in Milan,* which, although rooted in the reality of the slums of the city (a landlord tries to evict his tenants after oil is discovered on the land), takes off in flights of satiric fantasy. A delightful film and one of De Sica's best, it also measured the distance already opened up since the agonies of war's end. De Sica and Rossellini both went on to other, and in some cases forlornly inferior, achievements in later years, until De Sica did *The Garden of the Finzi-Continis* (1970) and, not long before his death, *A Brief Vacation* (1974), an angry piece of social observation written by Cesare Zavattini, his early collaborator on *Shoeshine* and *The Bicycle Thief.*

As the excitements of neorealism waned, an exciting and influential new (though not necessarily young) generation of filmmakers came to prominence in France. They were handily but inaccurately grouped as the New Wave (*La Nouvelle Vague*), as if they shared common aspirations for film, which they did not. They were alike only in that many of them had come to filmmaking from film criticism.

What the wave of French films (and there was *that*) dramatized in American/Holly-

De Sica's Umberto D *dramatized the plight of the aged—friendless, moneyless, helpless.*

The French influence on postwar cinema came from humanist films like Francois Truffaut's first feature, The 400 Blows, *with Jean-Pierre Léaud as a troubled teenager.*

wood eyes was the autonomy and the individuality of the director. The men now making films had as critics enunciated and expounded the *auteur* theory—the director as the author of his works, whether or not he had actually written the scripts. (Most of the American directors enshrined as *auteurs* by the French *auteuristes* did not in fact write their own scripts, but for the critics it was the visual or spiritual signature that mattered.) Now the critics were unquestionably *auteurs* in their

own right, and indeed they were in most cases the co-authors if not the sole authors of their scripts, as well as the directors and frequently the producers, too. European producers, unlike American producers, tended to be either silent and creatively powerless finance men or what Hollywood would consider production managers.

The Italian films offered a new kind of honesty; the French films offered what Hollywood with its committees and its assembly-line approach had almost always denied—a totally free creative hand for the director. The consequences of the new wave of freedom have been some of the most engrossing (and dissimilar) motion-picture viewing on American screens since the late 1950s. The French explored their uncommon ground as impressively as the Italians, and found a common esthetic in the trials of postwar recovery.

The 1959 Cannes Film Festival proved to be a kind of coronation ceremony for the New Wave. François Truffaut was voted best director for his first feature, *The 400 Blows*, his partly autobiographical portrait of a troubled teenager (whose growth and growing happiness he was to dramatize in several later films). Alain Resnais took the International Critics Prize for his intricately presented love story, *Hiroshima Mon Amour*, with its weavings of war-scarred pasts and present desires. Marcel Camus won the Grand Prix for *Black Orpheus*.

Claude Chabrol had won the foreign-language Oscar in 1958 for *Le Beau Serge*, which signifcantly resembled the neorealist films in its use of actual locations (Chabrol's own village), its combining of nonactors with professionals, and its examination of ordinary lives in a real environment. His story explored the interrelationships of two lifelong friends and the women in their lives. Preserving his gift for conveying the feeling and effects of surroundings, he moved toward stories of crimi-

Filming an homage to film, Truffaut directs Day for Night, *which also saluted Orson Welles, one of his idols, along with Hitchcock. Truffaut played a director making a film (which looked dreadful).*

nal passion, as in his subtle and stunning adaptation of Nicholas Blake's *The Beast Must Die* (1969).

The diverse interests of the French filmmakers were further displayed in the increasingly political work of Jean-Luc Godard in the 1960s, who moved from the dazzling inventions of *A Bout de Souffle* (Breathless) to the savageries of *Weekend* and the preachings of *La Chinoise*, which predicted the student uprisings of 1968.

Louis Malle has created a body of work uniquely diversified within itself, from the madcap adventures of *Zazie dans le Metro* to the wild adventure *Viva Maria*, co-starring Brigitte Bardot and Jeanne Moreau; a gentle story of an incestuous moment in *Murmur of the Heart*; a monumental documentary, *Phantom India*; and a probing look at a brutish peasant boy who becomes a French collaborator with the Gestapo, *Lacombe, Lucien*.

The originating ties among the New Wave filmmakers were a desire to work freely, inexpensively, and simply, independent of the encumbrances and interferences of major productions, plus an infatuation with the movies (which included American movies and espe-

cially the off-brands and B pictures, as well as the work of such French predecessors as the Jeans—Vigo, Cocteau, Renoir). Their early films were full of references, borrowings, and homages (a director's name chalked on a fence, cinema marquees for John Ford westerns). In time, their individuality separated the directors further, but the infatuation with movies remained, capped in 1973 by Truffaut's charming tribute to moviemaking, *Day for Night*, with its dream sequence celebrating Orson Welles and *Citizen Kane*.

The American movie marketplace was shrinking, but at least through the end of the 1960s it was also growing significantly more international than it had ever been. From Scandinavia have come the matchless soul-plumbings of Ingmar Bergman, whose work commands large audiences who are intrigued rather than put off by the privacy of the somber mood of some of the films.

England, like Italy, enjoyed a splendid if too short film renaissance, first with a succession of the best light comedies in modern times, featuring Alec Guinness or Peter Sellers or both, and then shifting into a superb run of social dramas (echoing the stage excitements beginning with John Osborne's *Look Back in Anger*). England found its own new wave in men like John Schlesinger (*Billy Liar, Darling, Far from the Madding Crowd, Sunday, Bloody Sunday*), Clive Donner (*Nothing But the Best, Here We Go Round the Mulberry Bush*), Tony Richardson (*Look Back in Anger, A Taste of Honey, The Loneliness of the Long-Distance Runner, Tom Jones*), Bryan Forbes (*Only Two Can Play, The L-Shaped Room*), and Lindsay Anderson (*This Sporting Life, If . . . , O Lucky Man*). Although generally operating within a production system much like Hollywood's—and in fact often partly or wholly financed by Hollywood in the postwar period—the British directors rigorously sought and got the creative in-

dependence that looked so enviable from the corner of Hollywood and Vine.

From the flow of superb films produced in the peacetime flowering of British and Continental cinema, it became clear that there could be more to the movies than Hollywood had dared dream of, and that the men to make them best were not the master-minding moguls but the creators themselves. There were barriers to full freedom of expression on the screen, anchored in the past and in law, but they were eroding fast.

And under the pressures of changing morality and falling revenues, the traditional studio hierarchies were eroding, creating a climate in which the lessons from the European experience could be acted upon in Hollywood. The inoculation was being absorbed and beginning to work.

By the later 1970s, with the event pictures, large and loud, dominating the Hollywood scene, a new European transfusion was needed—a fresh reminder that a humanist concern for the individual and relationships between individuals is part of the movie experience too. But in the 1950s there were other perils, other needs.

Young Britons rebelling at a boarding school in Lindsay Anderson's surrealist If . . . , *a late triumph of England's postwar cinema.*

45

The frightened fifties

Writing in the *New York Times* in 1949, Samuel Goldwyn, the great independent among the Hollywood patriarchs, looked into the future with sharp-eyed accuracy and an optimism not many of his peers shared. (Lester Markel of the *Times* was an uncredited collaborator, ut the energy, originality, and aptness of thought are manifestly all Goldwyn's.)

"Even the most backward-looking of the topmost tycoons of our industry cannot now help seeing just around the corner a titanic struggle to retain audiences," Goldwyn wrote. "The competition we feared in the past . . . will fade into insignificance by comparison with the fight we are going to have to keep people patronizing our theaters in preference to sitting home and watching a program of entertainment. It is a certainty that people will be unwilling to pay to see poor pictures when they can stay home and see something which is, at least, no worse."

He added, "If the movies try to lick television, it is the movies that will catch the licking." He was sure that a large segment of the industry would in time be making movies especially for television while another segment continued to make them for theaters, and he confidently predicted that pay television would be a boon for Hollywood. There would be no room "for the deadwood of the present or the faded glories of the past. . . . But no one in our industry who has real talent need fear the effects of television."

Goldwyn was right all the way, although it has taken a quarter of a century to see how prophetic he was. The titanic struggle to retain audiences, then just beginning, has never ended.

In the 1950s, in the days of television's lusty infancy, Hollywood fought back by doing what it did best and what television could not do as well, or at all. There were fewer pictures, but the biggest of them were really, really big. And while the Hays Code remained intact and honored, a few movies began to have an unaccustomed bite, such as *Born Yesterday*, with Judy Holliday's salty portrait of a junk dealer's dumb-blonde mistress who smartens up, and

Going out with a flourish, the movie musical, by the 1950s a financially endangered species, reached new heights in Vincente Minnelli's An American in Paris, *starring Gene Kelly.*

Billy Wilder's *Sunset Boulevard*, with William Holden as a kept man dancing and dying to the tune of a flamboyantly crazy silent star played by Gloria Swanson. Released in 1950, both films helped launch a last great dozen years of the Hollywood that was.

The Hollywood high style had never seemed more variously dazzling than in some of the 1951 films: Gene Kelly's brilliant choreographic explorations in *An American in Paris*; George Stevens's meticulous mounting of *A Place in the Sun*, with Elizabeth Taylor and Montgomery Clift as star-crossed lovers; John Huston's *The African Queen*, teaming Humphrey Bogart and Katharine Hepburn in extraordinary characterizations colliding amidst the suspenseful events scripted by James Agee from the C. S. Forester novel. That year, there was also Marlon Brando's intense triumph in *A Streetcar Named Desire* and Fredric March's astonishing and sobering portrait of a defeated man, Willy Loman, in Arthur Miller's *Death of a Salesman*, made by Stanley Kramer.

Many of the memorable films surviving from the 1950s have a dramatic power rooted in social realism, but it was sheer spectacle that the studio tycoons seized on as their best weapon against television. The rousing success of Cecil B. deMille's star-filled *The Greatest Show on Earth*, with its great train wreck and fiery climax, confirmed this conviction.

Indeed the traditional size and shape of the screen no longer seemed adequate to meet competitive needs. Two films in 3D, *Bwana Devil* and *House of Wax*, drew crowds and notoriety in 1953, but the tinted glasses were a nuisance and 3D quickly looked like what it was—a novelty but not a breakthrough.

Cinerama 52, which used three projectors to fill a vastly wide curved screen and to give at least an intermittent illusion of depth, had

A star of the past, Gloria Swanson made a dazzling return as a rather mad silent movie queen in Billy Wilder's Sunset Boulevard.

A star of the future (overleaf), Marlon Brando made a stunning debut in Streetcar.

48

enjoyed phenomenal business for its travel shots and roller-coaster ride. The need for three cameras and projectors, and having to match seams where the images joined, were bothersome. But width was a way to go and there began a battle of wide-screen processes.

Twentieth Century-Fox struck first with Cinemascope, which used a so-called anamorphic lens (developed years before by a French inventor named Henri Chrétien) to compress wider images into the normal 35mm frame of a film. The frame is customarily about one and a third times as wide as it is high. During projection, the same frames, shot with Cinemascope lenses, could be "unsqueezed" to produce images that were two and a third or two and a half times as wide as they were high, depending on the soundtrack system. In either system, Cinemascope was wide, wide, wide.

The studio quietly spent millions developing the camera and other equipment and persuading exhibitors throughout the country and the world to invest in the costly new screens and projectors Cinemascope required. (The projection lenses alone originally cost $2,500 each.) Fox also spent millions on its first Cinemascope spectacular, *The Robe*, and the gamble paid off. *The Robe* was a box-office smash, although it lost out to *From Here to Eternity* as best picture in 1953. The Motion Picture Academy voted a special award to Cinemascope and Class I scientific awards (Oscars) to Professor Chrétien, his aides, and the Fox technicians who had perfected the system. Fred Waller, who had developed Cinerama (it was used as a gunnery training device during the war), was also honored by the Academy that year. The industry's gratitude was heartfelt.

Paramount had thought 3D would be the shape of the future and was furious at having been outguessed. It quickly came up with its own wide-screen process, Vista Vision, which ran the film past the camera lens horizontally. The technique was cumbersome and created problems in sound reproduction. The studio used it for *White Christmas* and a few other titles, and then dropped the process.

Mike Todd, who had been an investor in Cinerama but who had sold his interest, approached American Optical to come up with a single-lens wide-screen process. The result was Todd-AO, which used 70mm film and in which he made his blockbusting, forty-four-star Jules Verne epic, *Around the World in 80 Days,* in 1956.

MGM then commissioned Panavision, a new firm that had developed a much less expensive substitute for the anamorphic lens required for Cinemascope, to produce still another, better, anamorphic system. "Metro gave us the run of the studio," says Panavision president Robert Gottschalk. The resulting Panavision system, available in both 35mm and 70mm, has survived to become the most widely used wide-screen system, as close students of the opening credits on current movies will have noticed.

The denouement of the race to swing wide is an interesting chapter within the Hollywood story. The Cinemascope cameras were bulky and hard to use in action sequences on location. But for sensitive performers, the lenses had a far more grievous defect: they made faces fat in close-ups. Audrey Hepburn had protested after some tests on *Roman Holiday*. MGM had naturally embraced Panavision; Columbia, the Mirisch Company, and other major producing companies had followed. Fox had just as naturally held out. Then Frank Sinatra, starring in *Von Ryan's Express* for Fox in Italy, rebelled when he saw the results of the first day's shooting. At his insistence, Panavision equipment was used instead of Cinemascope for the rest of the film. It was released without crediting either camera system, but Panavision's Gottschalk had

Duelling television, Mike Todd's Around the World in 80 Days *used a Gee Whiz cast led by David Niven as Phineas Fogg, here momentarily up against John Carradine.*

figured the word would get around town, and it did. Subsequently William Wyler (on *How to Steal a Million*) and Robert Wise (on *The Sand Pebbles*) insisted that Fox let them use Panavision. Richard Zanuck, by then—the 1960s—head of production at Fox, studied some comparative footage, decided that Cinemascope had had its day, and scuttled it. The process was gone, but the wide screen had come to stay (presenting television with problems of cropping images to fit television screens, and offering the home viewer such occasional delights as profiled noses talking to each other with eyes and ears lost beyond the edges of the tube).

The big picture had not, as it happened, solved Hollywood's problems, but the early novelty of it went so well that in February 1955 *Fortune* ran an article on Hollywood's comeback. (The Academy gratefully gave scientific awards to Todd-AO in 1957 and Panavision in 1958.) A string of large, and large-grossing, movies in the mid-fifties included the lovely *Lili, Three Coins in the Fountain,* Disney's 20,000 *Leagues Under the Sea, East of Eden* with new star James Dean, *The King and I, The Ten Commandments, Giant, The Bridge on the River Kwai,* and William Wyler's remake of *Ben Hur,* which won eleven Oscars.

In even larger images Hollywood could do what it had always done surpassingly well. Yet, after recovering from the first shock of television's arrival, total box-office revenues began to drop sharply again in the late 1950s. Attendance in 1954 had been half of what it was eight years earlier, and it was still dropping.

RKO, one of the major studios, which produced such classics as the Astaire-Rogers musicals and *Citizen Kane,* was bought in 1955 by General Tire, which devised "Million Dollar Movie" for its station WOR-TV in New York. The sale of movies to television, which had earlier been resisted by the studios, began

Disney, too, joined the move to live action spectaculars, with James Mason as Captain Nemo in 20,000 Leagues Under the Sea *and Kirk Douglas, Peter Lorre and Paul Lukas in deep with him amidst fine special effects,*

in a panicky rush for needed cash. By one
estimate, nearly 2,000 features were made
available to television in the first half of 1956,
including almost 800 MGM movies made between 1929 and 1949.

The moguls were departing from an unset-
tled scene. Louis B. Mayer died in 1957, only

six years after he had been forced out of the
studio he built. Harry Cohn, the irascible and
strong-willed founder of Columbia, died in
1958 and so did Harry Warner, leaving Jack
Warner in sole command of the studio the
brothers had started in 1921. (Warner re-
sponded to the changing times with an agility

worthy of a founding entrepreneur. Warner's had a succession of undistinguished but popular and long-running television series, including "77 Sunset Strip" and several slightly changed variants. And with *Who's Afraid of Virginia Woolf?* Jack Warner, as we shall see, not only anticipated the trend of the movies, but helped bring a new day closer.)

If the spectaculars were fresh assertions of the movie past, there were already in the 1950s glimmerings of alternate currents, glimpses of other creative possibilities.

Elia Kazan's melodramatic *On the Waterfront* in 1954, with a tough script by Budd Schulberg and another memorable performance by Marlon Brando, this time as a sweet, slow-witted dock worker eager to be a champion but betrayed by his crooked brother, foreshadowed a newer Hollywood vision of life. Here, if poetic justice for the moment still prevailed, the good guy did not necessarily win and evil was understood to persist.

Good triumphed in two other fine films, Stanley Kramer's *High Noon* (1952) and John Sturges's *Bad Day at Black Rock* (1954), starring Spencer Tracy as a one-armed war veteran who takes on and defeats a corrupt town to avenge the murder of a Nisei comrade. Tracy, acting alone, and Gary Cooper, forced to act alone by the cowardice of the good citizens of his town, made classic reluctant heroes, but it is the embodiment of evil (and the possibility of weakness in numbers), that we remember now as having given those films their lingering reverberations.

Amidst all the epics, the quiet modesty of Delbert Mann's *Marty* in 1955 was startling. The sentimental realism of Paddy Chayevsky's story about the tongue-tied courtship of a shy Bronx butcher (Ernest Borgnine) and a shy and equally lonely schoolteacher (Betsy Blair) was a tonic change from superheated heroics. It was voted the year's best picture by the Academy, which was mildly surprising not be-

Epic tradition survived well in David Lean's Bridge on the River Kwai, *with Alec Guinness brilliant as a defiant captured British officer.*

56

The young Marlon Brando was unforgettable as a nice guy betrayed by his brother (Rod Steiger, right) and Lee J. Cobb in On the Waterfront.

cause of its merits, which were obvious, but because *Marty* represented the beginning of the counterinvasion of the movies by television. It had been done originally as a television drama. Chayevsky and Mann were the first of a whole generation of writers and directors groomed in live-television drama to score a significant triumph in the movies.

The Breen Office, which administered the Hays Code, began to seem even more like a besieged camp trying to hold off irresistible change. Some minor softenings of the old

taboos had been made in 1950, but they satisfied almost no one. In many movies there was a challenging boldness that defied the spirit even if it observed the specifics of the Code, while leaving no doubt that steamy, untidy, and unruly passions were part of the human spirit.

Picnic (1955), with William Holden as a wandering stud set loose amid the stifled and frustrated sexuality of a Midwestern town, caught the frenzy of passion answered and the humiliation of passion spurned with a candor that did not need to be graphic to be convincing. Tennessee Williams's *The Rose Tattoo*, also from 1955, used the high-ferocity talents of Anthony Quinn and Anna Magnani to convey his crackling romantic drama.

Billy Wilder's eccentric and inventive comedy, *Some Like It Hot* (1959), with Jack Lemmon and Tony Curtis in drag, fleeing mobsters and pursuing sax-playing sex symbol Marilyn Monroe, took neither its heterosexual nor its transvestite jokes seriously. But this film's use of free-form carnality had a sophisticated confidence that was in its way a departure from the screen's long-standing inhibitions.

Despite the sweaty provocations of Carroll Baker as a thumb-sucking nymphet (a slightly senior nymphet by *Lolita* standards) in *Baby Doll* (1956), the Hollywood norm was more often sex as a noncontact sport. The issue was never more stylishly avoided than in the Rock Hudson–Doris Day *Pillow Talk* in 1959. The harder-eyed handling of sex was, in the fifties, still an imported commodity. Jack Clayton's *Room at the Top*, in which the late Laurence Harvey climbed from bed to better, was the frankest nonexploitive display of sex as weapon yet done (in 1959) in English, and the film's American success was not at all lost on Hollywood.

Gigi, the richly romantic Lerner and Loewe rendering of a Colette story, directed by Vincente Minnelli in 1958, was not the last of the great Hollywood musicals, but it ended colossally the particular tradition of the MGM musicals, which in their extravagant luxury have never been equalled. *Gigi*, appropriately, was a considerable but isolated success.

The lonely butcher, Marty, *became a folk hero, first on television, then played by Ernest Borgnine in a gentle film.*

The movies, as the fifties ended, were playing to fewer customers each year. Television was locking viewers in the living room with longer formats and enriched production values and, increasingly, with the recent best of Hollywood's own productions.

The significant sixties

No decade in the history of the movies has been without crisis, ranged on a scale from merely exacerbating to apparently apocalyptic. No decade in the life of a still-evolving medium has passed without leaving some significant change, usually for the better. The coming of sound in the late 1920s was a profound step forward. It enabled a medium that had conquered space and motion to explore more complicated themes and ideas, subtler shadings of character, wider ranges of emotion. I suspect that the sixties left movies more significantly reshaped and repositioned than any period since the coming of the talkies.

All the pressures toward revolutionary change set free by the end of World War II—the upsurge in alternative leisure-time activities, the birth and fantastic growth of television, the divorcing of the major studios from their captive theaters, the invasion of the foreign films with all their freshness and candor, the acknowledgment that as a society we

were quite different from the images we saw on American movie screens—had now been roiling together for a dozen years or more.

The movies, then as now, were a unique and abrasively linked twinship of art and commerce. Hollywood, seen in 20/20 hindsight, was caught in a tightening squeeze of its two sides, each demanding urgent and fundamental change—the executives determined to shore up the sagging balance sheets, the creators demanding that the art form be brought forward into a new day.

For once, the dollars-and-cents practicality of the men who financed the movies and the creative aspirations of the filmmakers could be seen in a common cause. But nothing in Hollywood is ever quite as simple as it seems. The industry's conventional wisdom, insisting that the way things have always been done is the way they always will be done, had an irresistible momentum and attraction. As in most industries, this is the first and last refuge of the uncertain and the insecure, and Holly-

Super spectacles, like David Lean's vivid Lawrence of Arabia, *with Peter O'Toole and Anthony Quinn, were the movie industry's principal counterthrust to television.*

wood, circa 1960, was a hotbed of uncertainty.

By the end of the decade, Hollywood was making films that would not have been dared in 1960 or even 1965. An X-rated movie (*Midnight Cowboy*) was honored as Best Picture of the Year in 1969 (and was applauded by national church groups, which in earlier times had been the strongest forces toward containment of the movies within a simple-minded propriety). Yet the revolution had taken place as an inevitable, gradual process, not by direct action.

The principal barrier to change—which had to be breached, and was—was the Production Code of the Motion Picture Association of America (MPAA), the organization of the major studios. Even now it is hard to realize quite what a finicky but dictatorial power the so-called Hays Code and its administrators held over American movies for more than thirty years. Most famously, the strictures of the Code against profanity necessitated solemn discussion and a once-only exception to allow Clark Gable as Rhett Butler to say, "Frankly, my dear, I don't give a damn" to Vivien Leigh as Scarlett O'Hara in *Gone With the Wind.*

The quick march toward a Code had started in the scandal-ridden Hollywood of the early 1920s. The death of a girl after an orgiastic night in San Francisco led to the indictment of comedian Fatty Arbuckle. Arbuckle was subsequently acquitted but his career was finished, and the acquittal did nothing to stop the noisy protests around the country about Hollywood's shenanigans, both off-screen and on.

There had always been fears about the movies' potentially corrupting powers. Chicago had passed an ordinance establishing a procedure for censoring films as early as 1907, and by the 1920s there were censorship boards in several cities and states. Harry Warner and the other studio bosses saw very clearly the

possibility of more censors and fewer customers as church leaders preached against the licentiousness rampant on the shores of the too-blue Pacific. Desperate to give the industry a tonier image, the Motion Picture Association recruited President Harding's postmaster general, a salty but rectitudinous Indiana politician named Will Hays, to be the industry's first czar, at a deeply respectable $100,000 a year.

The Code, written for Hays by Father Daniel J. Lord, S.J., and Martin Quigley, a Catholic layman who published an influential trade journal, was first adopted in March 1930. This was to be the set of guidelines that presumably would be followed by the member studios of the Association. But the Code did nothing to silence the outcries against the movies, particularly within the Catholic Church. When in April 1934 the hierarchy formed the Legion of Decency—with an already-demonstrated power to keep thousands of the faithful away from particular films—the Association within weeks passed a Resolution of Uniform Interpretation. It established a Production Code Administration to preview scripts before shooting as well as to view finished films. Without a final Seal of Approval from the Code Administration, no studio would distribute a movie or allow it to be shown in studio-owned theaters.

The idea, of course, was voluntary self-regulation as an alternative to imposed censorship from any level of government. And so long as the major studios controlled many hundreds of theaters throughout the United States, there was a strong economic reason for compliance. Given the temper of the times, the Code succeeded very satisfactorily in keeping the civil censors at bay. Why shouldn't it have? The Code was as stern as any but the most sanctimonious censor could have asked for. It ran to more than fifteen closely printed pages, from its first princi-

The scandal of Fatty Arbuckle, here seen sipping sweetly with Alice Lake, pushed the movies toward self-censorship. Accused of murder but acquitted, Arbuckle was ruined anyway.

ple—"No picture shall be produced which will lower the moral standards of those who see it"—through its specific prohibitions against obscenity and profanity to its cautions on the treatment of murder, crime, drugs, alcohol, costumes, religion, national feelings, and dancing. There were specific rules against films dealing with sex hygiene, venereal disease, and miscegenation. There could be no traveling-salesmen or farmer's-daughter jokes, and "the treatment of bedrooms must be governed by good taste and delicacy," said the Code.

The Code Administration came to be known as the Breen Office, after Joseph Breen, the tough and wily negotiator who ran it during its most potent years. As itemized as much of the Code was, it still needed in-

A steamy departure in Hollywood films, Baby Doll, starred Carroll Baker as a semi-innocent sexpot.

terpretation, precedents, and more and more specifics. A kiss, Breen & Company decided, was too incendiary if it went more than ten seconds. The liveliest and most revealing account of the workings of the office is given in *See No Evil* (Simon & Schuster, 1970) by Jack Vizzard, who was on the Administration staff. What emerges, along with the often gamy anecdotes of the cajolery and compromise by which the Code proceeded, is a sense of Vizzard's growing disillusionment with the rating process and his awareness of its inadequacy in the postwar world, even though it is also clear that he has little heart for much of what the movies are now permitted to offer.

The first really important defeat for the Code came with a bright, innocuous social comedy, *The Moon Is Blue*, made by Otto Preminger in 1952. The Administration, then headed by Breen's successor, Geoffrey Shurlock, denied the film a Seal of Approval, partly because of its use of such words as "virgin" but mostly because of the story's lighthearted view of extramarital dalliance. ("Adultery and Illicit Sex . . . must not be explicitly treated or justified, or presented attractively," the Code stated.) United Artists, which had financed the picture, was an old-line company now under new ownership and fighting back from the brink of bankruptcy. UA elected to defy the Code, released *The Moon Is Blue* without a Seal of Approval, and resigned from the Motion Picture Association. With all that tasty publicity to help it along, *The Moon Is Blue* (which was actually a bit less outspoken than the "Mary Tyler Moore Show") became a solid success at the box office. A Maryland court denied a suit that would have banned it in that state. A few years later, Shurlock quietly gave the film a Seal of Approval after all, and UA rejoined the Association.

The lesson was plain: with the theaters formerly controlled by the major studios now free to play any movie they could get, with or without a Seal, the lions guarding the Code were suddenly rendered toothless.

Preminger challenged the Code again in 1956 with Nelson Algren's *The Man with the Golden Arm*, in which Frank Sinatra played a Chicago card dealer with the thirty-five-pound monkey of narcotics addiction on his back. Narcotics were a forbidden theme under the Code, and UA once again released a movie without the Seal. The film remains one of Preminger's best, and even after a latter-day succession of drug-culture pictures, it is as harrowingly valid a study of addiction as we have had. On its merits, and aided by Saul Bass's striking titles and ad campaign, *The Man with the Golden Arm* was another Seal-free box-office hit. (If the movies had been free from the start to deal with addiction as honestly as Preminger did, one wonders whether the crisis of drug abuse in the last several years would have been lessened to any extent.)

Golden Arm didn't get its Seal, but *Baby Doll* did that same year, despite the sweaty sexual tensions that Elia Kazan generated around his suggestively hot-loined star, Carroll Baker. For once, the Code men were heavily attacked for being too lenient, and Francis Cardinal Spellman denounced the film as an occasion of sin and forbade Catholics to see it. *Baby Doll* did well despite the ban, doubtless because of all the notoriety, but it was far from being an exploitation film. Its sexuality existed in the whole context of a time, a place, and a condition of life. It was a long lope beyond the coy and chaste romancings in which kisses lasted a crisp ten seconds. While the film's shock value probably obscured its other strengths, it was a salty foretaste of the indelicate but credible handling of basic and blinding human emotions the movies were now reaching for.

Tentatively at first, the American films of the 1960s began to say, in one tone of voice or another, that life was not quite so tidy and neatly resolved as it might be. Billy Wilder's *The Apartment* (1960) was a sharp and expert comedy that, despite its upbeat ending (Jack Lemmon straining spaghetti through a tennis racket for his dinner with Shirley MacLaine),

Richard Brooks' Elmer Gantry, featuring Burt Lancaster as a fiery preacher, treated oldtime religion without oldtime sentiment.

acidly etched a portrait of executive-level adultery, amoral ambition, and male chauvinist swinery.

That same year Richard Brooks's *Elmer Gantry*, based on the Sinclair Lewis novel, was released. It demonstrated that a large-scale,

well-made, muscular Hollywood movie, climaxed by a spectacular fire, could also get to the black heart of character, exposing the lusts of a gaudy evangelist (fervently played by Burt Lancaster). Yet *Butterfield 8*, playing down much of the sexual drive John O'Hara had reported so graphically in his novel, seemed in its reticence more characteristic of a studio system still torn between tradition and change.

The moviemakers couldn't help noticing the change, because even though Hollywood's movies still dominated American theaters, they were more and more often sharing screen time with imported films, which were less restricted and whose audiences continued to grow. The chronicle of the 1960s is at once the coming of age of American films and the internationalizing of the American market, and each is part of the other.

There was the splendid, generally impersonal sheen of *Elmer Gantry*, let's say, with its characters writ larger than life, and the intimacy of *Never on Sunday*, made by the expatriate American director Jules Dassin and celebrating the healing powers of a warm-hearted Greek prostitute (played by Melina Mercouri). From England, the angry working-class drama by Karel Reisz, *Saturday Night and Sunday Morning*, seethed with both the vitality and the frustrations of ordinary lives. So, more quietly, did Jack Clayton's adaptation of D. H. Lawrence's *Sons and Lovers*.

Federico Fellini's *La Dolce Vita* in 1961 portrayed an Italy that had gone beyond recovery to satiety. Its star, Marcello Mastroianni, moving somberly through a night world of unfulfilling indulgence and anxious, undefined expectation, became an early symbol of the bored alienation and dissatisfaction that ran as a motif through later films made in almost every country in the Western world, including America.

Stanley Kubrick, a precocious, ambitious New Yorker who was a still photographer for *Look* magazine while in his teens and had subsequently made three strong and strongly individualistic features—*The Killing*, *Paths of Glory*, and *Spartacus*—in 1962 gave the old Code another push toward extinction with his adaptation of Vladimir Nabokov's novel *Lolita*. Nabokov had given the word "nymphet" a new currency. Sue Lyon, wearing oversized sunglasses and sucking an all-day lollipop, was Kubrick's nymphet, youthfully, innocently, fatefully attractive to James Mason, so hung up on his unrequited love that he married her oversexed mother just to be nearby.

It was a story that many thought could not be filmed. A few years earlier it might not have been possible, but films from abroad had effectively isolated the Code in all its anachronistic glory. Kubrick's film was shocking only in the *idea* that a middle-aged man could

The battle to keep Fox *from bankruptcy in the troubled Sixties was led by Darryl Zanuck, here swapping cigars with Robert Mitchum on location of* The Longest Day, *the all-star reenactment of the Normandy landings, which did save the studio.*

68

feel such an obsessive love for a downy-cheeked adolescent. (Indeed, Sue Lyon was a good three years older than the Lolita of Nabokov's perspiring dreams, which made the movie seem a bit less perverse than it might have.) The idea was swathed in black comedy dominated not by Mason, the nymphet, or Shelley Winters as her raucous mother, but by Peter Sellers as Quilty, Mason's nemesis, who gets Lolita but doesn't really want her.

With this bizarre entourage wending its way through America's motels and drive-ins, *Lolita* had strong elements of farce that spilled over into romantic triangulations. Yet in the postlude, when Mason's Humbert Humbert makes a last pilgrimage to see a Lolita who is now married and a mother, the jokes are over. In all his wretchedness, Humbert manifests a forlorn dignity, and Lolita, like a glittering star that has burned out prematurely, seems to have settled for the drabbest kind of domesticity.

The movie got its Seal, not without outcries from church leaders, who this time included Protestant theologian Reinhold Neibuhr. Yet in its circumspect handling of the theme, *Lolita* could hardly have been denied a Seal, certainly not if American films were going to retain any kind of creative equality with foreign films. The real importance of *Lolita* seems not so much its December-February romance as its personal, unconventional, uneven point of view—part Kubrick, part Nabokov. It was unquestionably an American film by an American director, but its assertive and quirky individuality was somehow on the European model. In that sense, *Lolita* sharply forecast the waning of the distinction between American and European movies, and of the Code, and of the studios themselves.

As the 1960s advanced, the movies no longer fit the tidy, enveloping images we once had for them. They were no longer a mosaic, varicolored but all in the same plane. They were no longer a spectrum spanning a rainbow from red to violet. What they were becoming—and still are—is a gallery, offering on the same shelves, so to speak, original Rembrandts and cheap reproductions, Goyas and comic books, Giacomettis and junk assemblages. There is a widening divergence in the levels of intention and in the filmmakers' presumptions about the taste and comprehension of the audiences. there is evidence of new leavenings in old formulas.

David Lean's *Lawrence of Arabia* in 1962 was a classic large-scale action spectacular. Lean and screenwriter-playwright Robert Bolt also tried to depict, in a gingerly fashion on an intimate scale, Lawrence's complexity and sexual confusion. Another spectacular, Darryl F. Zanuck's vast re-creaion of the invasion of Europe, *The Longest Day*, was treated in an entirely traditional and straightforward manner. (The film also rescued Twentieth Century-Fox from the verge of bankruptcy and returned Zanuck to the leadership of the studio.)

Days of Wine and Roses, directed by Blake Edwards and released in 1962, with Jack Lemmon and Lee Remick as husband-and-wife alcoholics, was even more devastating in its look at the perils of overdrink than *The Lost Weekend* had been a few years earlier. It offered even less consoling hope that both its protagonists would find their way back to sobriety; the guess was that at least one of them never would.

No one is likely to accuse 1963 of being a major vintage year for movies. It was a time of replanting, and the variety of its offerings is revealing. Tony Richardson's *Tom Jones* was the most uninhibited fun in a very long time; its famous, sexually suggestive eating scene between Albert Finney and a comely wench (Joyce Redman) gave fried chicken a new lease on life. For all its innuendos, it swashbuckled its way past the censors without

The generation gap between James Mason and Sue Lyon in Stanley Kubrick's Lolita *took the movies deeper into sexuality.*

trouble. If anybody in 1962 had wanted benchmarks to measure the breadth of movie intentions, they were conveniently at hand in *This Sporting Life* and *Cleopatra*. Lindsay Anderson's portrait of the world of a kind, brooding, inarticulate professional rugby player (played with both muscle and delicacy by Richard Harris) and the embittered landlady (Rachel Roberts) he glumly loved was claustrophobically intense, frugal with speech,

lavish with dark moods. *Cleopatra* was, well, *Cleopatra*, a spectacle to end them all, as it nearly ended Fox, but finally a better film on its own splashy terms than all its production problems would have led you to expect.

Even *Cleopatra* presented the Code with minor sweats: how much of Elizabeth Taylor's asp-bitten breast could tastefully be revealed? As Joseph Mankiewicz had thoughtfully kept his camera at a respectful distance, however, all was well.

Indeed, given the swift evolution of public attitudes and a certain weariness among those administering the Code, it might have been

abandoned a few years sooner than it actually was. Eric Johnston, a suave diplomat who had followed Will Hays as head of the MPAA in 1945, died in 1963 and for three crucial years no one who seemed suitable could be found to replace him. The Code bumped along. In 1964, it bumped into Billy Wilder's amusingly cynical tale of an accidental one-night, two-couple confrontation, *Kiss Me Stupid*. The Code office approved the film, which was probably a fair decision if not a prudent one. Wilder was not really glorifying infidelity, although he dared to be amused rather than horrified by the fact that it does take place more often than once in a while. The public reaction to the film was surprisingly harsh, and even some of the critics joined in the denunciations of Wilder. The force of the negative response to *Kiss Me Stupid* was a numbing shock to him and his writing partner, I. A. L. Diamond. Years later, discussing it over a lunch at Goldwyn Studios, they were still baffled at their gross misreading of public taste. Part of the reason may have been that their film was released in the same season as *My Fair Lady* and *Mary Poppins*. Wilder proved, in any event, that it is always possible to get a little too far ahead of community tolerances, even when they are relaxing fast.

When, in May 1966, Jack Valenti was named president of the MPAA, the question of the Production Code was near the top of his agenda of long-deferred and urgent business. Valenti, a graduate of the Harvard Business School, had worked in a Dallas ad agency before becoming a White House aide to President Johnson. ("I sleep better at night knowing Lyndon Johnson is my president," Valenti said. "I sleep better through movies, knowing Jack Valenti is my president," Stan Freberg announced at one of the first banquets Valenti attended in Hollywood).

Wily old Jack Warner had seen Edward Albee's *Who's Afraid of Virginia Woolf?* on

its opening night in New York in 1963 and quickly bought the screen rights. The Code men had written out most of the profanities Albee had written in. By 1966 Warner had filmed the play, not much changed at all, with Mike Nichols directing and Elizabeth Taylor and Richard Burton co-starring as the faculty couple corroding in their own despair. There was simply no way the sense and sound of Albee's work could be preserved within the strictures of the Code, yet Warner had no intention of gutting his movie. He was seventy-four but his pioneering days were not over. When the Seal was denied, he dictated his own compromise. He made a few minor changes in language, labeled the film "Suggested for Mature Audiences," and insisted that theaters showing the film police their box offices and deny admission to those under eighteen unless they were accompanied by their parents.

It was an interim solution, gratefully accepted by Valenti on behalf of the Code Administration. This compromise was used again in 1966 on two important English films, Lewis Gilbert's *Alfie* and Silvio Narrizzano's *Georgy Girl*. The problem in *Alfie* was not Michael Caine's portrayal of a raffish and amoral romancer, but a backroom abortion scene with Vivien Merchant as the patient and Denholm Elliott as the doctor. The scene, harrowing to remember a decade later, was cruel but crucial to the film. It was included not as a glorification but as a reality of life. The single girl's life was explored in *Georgy Girl* as Lynn Redgrave tried to better her gawky, endearing self. The "Suggested for Mature Audiences" tags for the first time officially acknowledged the new truth about the movies: they were no longer necessarily made for a single vast audience; they might, in fact, be inappropriate for an "immature" patron, no matter how much past twenty-one he or she might happen to be.

The super spectacular Cleopatra *made Elizabeth Taylor the costliest screen queen in history. Later Liz and the movies turned to a different kind of spectacle (next page).*

Who's Afraid of Virginia Woolf? which came along first and most noisily, was a film of landmark significance. Today its language—"God damn you" and "hump the hostess"—fails to have shock value and is not even cut on television. But in July 1966 it was shocking. More than the language, the film's vision of a marriage—in fact, two marriages—was startling. Before this, no movie had ever shown anything quite like the destructive frenzy of George and Martha, each tearing the other apart, screaming and taunting and drinking and embroiling a younger couple (who had numerous problems of their own) as pawns in their wars of emotional attrition. Even so, it was possible to see *Virginia Woolf* as a love story, to find George and Martha a couple lashed together by needs they hated to acknowledge but could not deny. If indeed there were glimpses of love lurking beyond the squalls of venom and thunders of contempt, it was the foreground that riveted one's attention—the unprecedented acting-out of rage, frustration, and degradation, a trip to the lower depths of the soul.

It was all that, and it was mainstream, commercial, major-studio Hollywood, with almost the last of the founding fathers presiding proudly over an important new director and a pair of stars who had never before performed with such lacerating force.

It was, as Warner knew it would be, the beginning of a different era in American movies, perhaps not to be compared with the sound era, which his studio had ushered in, but a new era nevertheless. A year earlier Warner had said, "I'm against gutter stuff, as everybody knows, but the improvement in what you can do in good taste is gigantic." He had no illusions that every film that followed would be made with the care of *Virginia Woolf*, but that was the risk. "You can't stand still," he said.

A landmark, Who's Afraid of Virginia Woolf? *with Elizabeth Taylor, Richard Burton, George Segal, and Sandy Dennis spending a hellish night together, set new and freer standards for movie theme and language.*

You can't, and American movies haven't. In the wake of *Virginia Woolf* came a small procession of films that explored the human condition with a candor and confidence not possible before.

Michelangelo Antonioni's *Blow-Up* (American-financed by MGM) was not to everyone's taste in 1967. If you weren't with it, it was full of pretentious symbolism and fashionable theatrics. But if you went along with Antonioni's remarkable impressionism, *Blow-*

Further developments in movie freedom came with Antonioni's Blow-Up *and David Hemmings adrift amidst teenyboppers in swinging London.*

Up was a dead-accurate summoning-up of most of the moving parts in swinging London. The city's new elite of up-from-Cockney artists, costumers, hair stylists, and chic photographers was nicely telescoped into David Hemmings as the picture-taking protagonist, romping with a brace of naked birds (whose display of pubic hair gave the Code fits and, until it was removed from view, caused the movie to be banned in London). The film's central uncertainty—had Hemmings seen a murder, and were there clues in his photographic enlargements?—seemed indeed symbolic, or symptomatic of a cultural climate in which there were no longer many sure, fixed values. Fashion and fashions changed between five and seven o'clock, and the in-ness of people, places, and things was trickier to chart than a game of backgammon. But the world—potty, casual, permissive, vaguely sad in its affluence and bored in its freedom from commitment—was all there in *Blow-Up*, and its abrasions, while less obvious, were more worrisome than pubic hair.

The uses of the new freedom were variously and indelibly revealed that same year in Arthur Penn's *Bonnie and Clyde* and Mike Nichols's *The Graduate*. In a sense, Penn's treatment of the real Bonnie Parker and Clyde Barrow was a kind of high-gloss glorifying—a romanticizing, certainly—of a couple of criminals. (The Code men in an earlier time might have been disapproving, even though Bonnie and Clyde finally got their just desserts.) The original Robert Benton-David Newman script had dealt more extensively than the resulting movie with the fairly complicated sexuality of Bonnie, Clyde, and others in their gang. Penn and his producer-star, Warren Beatty, chose to drop much of it. They preserved, with careful and oblique references, Clyde's impotence as one clue to his impulsive and showy crimes and later as a causative factor in his ripening love for Bonnie.

The movie—in my view still one of the half-dozen finest to come out of America in the last ten years—mixed rough comedy and bloody tragedy with supple skill. If Bonnie and Clyde were romanticized beyond the reach of truth, it had been so in their own time, and what Penn did so well was to play off their airy charm and their growing love against the downward and darkening spiral of their lives—the joyrides getting grimmer, the wounds more serious, the motels greasier, the pursuit more relentless. The last sylvan interlude is the cruelest illusion of all, the glimpse of the lost alternative.

The Graduate, released at the end of 1967, was one of those social comedies that catches the main currents of a generation's thought more accurately and prophetically than sociology or sermon. Buck Henry's script, adapted from a novel by Charles Webb, reflected the dissatisfactions that whole regiments of Dustin Hoffmans and Katharine Rosses were feeling with the aspirations and contentments of their elders. The elders were not necessarily ecstatic, and Anne Bancroft's Mrs. Robinson survives as a comic yet tragic symbol of the never-satisfied acquisitive romantic instinct in many middle-class matrons.

The relationship between the graduate and Mrs. Robinson, which would have been unacceptable and unworkable on several grounds under the original Code, managed to be operationally hilarious, then uncomfortably unattractive, and at last a horror of inevitable consequences. *The Graduate* was a comedy of substance as well as of bad manners; the charm of its stars could not conceal a cold core of reality. Few seemingly happy endings have in fact played so chill and ambiguous as Hoffman and Ross, she still in her wedding gown, riding off God knows where on a city bus. Nichols holds the wordless shot for what seems an eternity, the smiles growing fixed and something like alarm creeping in behind the eyes. A clinical coolness marks all of his work, and in *The Graduate* Nichols left little doubt that at the end of the bus line some hard and unfunny decisions had to be made —options to hang in there and think seriously about plastics or drop out and become tomorrow's easy rider.

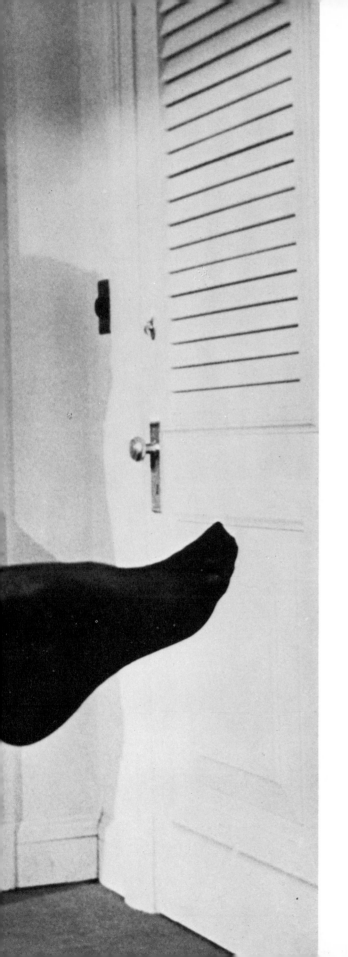

I once asked Nichols if he had ever speculated on what the next scene would have been. He had "They ride along for another five minutes," he said thoughtfully, "and then she leaps up and says, 'My God, I haven't got a thing to wear!'"

Richard Brooks's *In Cold Blood* (1967) deployed the screen's new maturity in another direction. Drawn from Truman Capote's massive reportage, first serialized in *The New Yorker* and then published as a book, Brooks's film was impressionistic but documentary-like in meticulously controlled black and white. It explored the fated-from-birth lives of the two men who slaughtered the defenseless Clutters, a Kansas farm family. Book and movie were acts of advocacy against capital punishment, and the movie's last sounds, the dying heartbeats of one of the hanged killers, carried the horror of yet another killing done in (official) cold blood. The slaughter and the boys' failure-ridden lives were depicted with insistent graphic honesty. We were made witnesses to truth, and it hurt to a degree that films had not often hurt us.

Stanley Kramer's *Guess Who's Coming to Dinner?* will probably survive in memory as the final tremulous teaming of Spencer Tracy and Katharine Hepburn. But in 1967 it was also a landmark film thematically. The presence of its superstars and the well-lit, well-furnished, clean-cut middle-class movie tradition in which the film was made helped to mellow the message. The characters, drawn large and clear, included Sidney Poitier as a world-famous doctor deeply in love with the daughter of Tracy and Hepburn played by Hepburn's niece Katharine Houghton. The parents, acknowledging and warning the young people about the social perils of a marriage between black and white, nevertheless gave it their blessing. What had been unthinkable under the 1934 Code had become a thinkable, recognizable fact of life. The film

*A serious comedy about changing social values, Mike Nichols' *The Graduate *had Dustin Hoffman succumbing to Mrs. Robinson (Anne Bancroft).*

was not banned anywhere and played throughout the United States with only two or three overt incidents, all in the urban North. The critical, and even some audience, complaints were that the handling of the material was too old-fashioned, reticent, and idealized. "Why," said a black actor sardonically, "couldn't Sidney have been a simple country doctor from Scarsdale?" The movies were changing; the times were changing even faster.

There was in the late 1960s one final, annihilating assault on the Code that had been safeguarding our moral values since 1934. It was obvious to Jack Valenti that the "Suitable for Mature Audiences" compromise arrived at in mid-1966 was not a permanent solution. Its two alternatives (a film was presumably either "mature" or "not mature") were inadequate to characterize all the emerging categories of films.

After months of planning and adroit politicking, in November 1968 Valenti unveiled a brand-new system of ratings which, with a couple of minor changes in nomenclature, is still in use. The categories are: G (suitable for everyone); PG (parental guidance suggested); R (restricted—no one under seventeen admitted unless accompanied by parent or guardian); and X (no one under eighteen admitted at all).

In theory the ratings ought to be of little or no interest to the critic contemplating the art under the guise of eternity. But the truth is that the new system, for all its inaccuracies and imperfections, has potentially opened up the screen to the ultimate coming of age of film as an art form in the sense that creative filmmakers need no longer concern themselves with an abstract set of moral criteria.

Philosophically, the system goes to the heart of film's new position in the society; it acknowledges that each film is no longer addressed to every person in an audience, that

A serious social issue was lightly handled in Guess Who's Coming to Dinner, *about the interracial love between Katharine Hepburn's daughter and Sidney Poitier, as a world famous doctor.*

Sweet surrender, no longer banned in film, still gave spinster Joanne Woodward qualms in James Olson's arms in Rachel, Rachel.

in effect film is a pluralistic medium in a pluralistic society. The system replaces the old punitive and negative approach, with its catalogue of don'ts, and substitutes for it a reliance on the responsibility and good judgment of the filmmaker. The underlying notion is that the ratings are an early-warning system aimed principally at parents. The creator, says the system, has the right to free expression; the public, however, also has the right to be forewarned that some movies are more incendiary than others. The pragmatic hope is that a voluntary system will discourage official censorship and harassing court suits over specific films, triggered by feelings that nobody is really watching the store.

Valenti skillfully engineered the participation in the new system not only of his own group, the MPAA, but also of the exhibitors and the foreign-film distributors. While the

Linking old and new, enduring star John Wayne gently parodied himself in True Grit, *helping Kim Darby and earning an Oscar.*

PG category was purely cautionary, the R and X categories promised a policing of the box office, which the theatermen indeed agreed to do.

The X category is, in theory, the area where voluntary compliance meets law enforcement. Admitting anyone who is under eighteen years old to an X-rated film might well be cause for legal action, so it is no wonder that the ticket booths at X-rated films are carefully watched. What is more surprising is that, even though the policing of the box office at R-rated movies has been inconsistent, it has

been attended to well enough to avoid widespread complaints.

The ratings have been resoundingly attacked for their bloopers which have been proportionately few but disproportionately conspicuous. *True Grit* (1969) was G-rated despite a scene in which one man slices off another's finger, and another long sequence in which a helpless, terrified girl is attacked by a rattlesnake. Sam Peckinpah's spectacularly violent *The Getaway* (1972) was given a PG. *Scalawag* (1973), directed by Kirk Douglas, was strewn with violent death (however bloodlessly it was depicted) and first rated PG; Douglas appealed and the film was finally given a G rating. It made little difference because the family audience for which the film was intended simply found it too violent. David Lean's *Ryan's Daughter* (1970), on the other hand, first drew an R rating because of an innocuous love scene. When MGM appealed, the rating was changed to PG, which may have been fair but which suggested that the system was vulnerable to big-studio pressures, as well as being over-sensitive to sex and under-sensitive to violence.

The mild PG rating given to Universal's *Jaws* in 1975 struck me as wrong and misleading. Studies have shown that children are most strongly affected by screen violence done to or threatening other children, and the easy rating seemed an insufficient warning to parents that Peter Benchley's giant shark maims and devours children as well as grownups. The studio, having fought for the PG, ran its own cautionary note in the *Jaws* ads (where of course it can be taken as either a warning or an incitement).

Most of the rating controversies have involved a similar permissiveness toward violence, although both language and sexual themes have been at issue. In 1976 *All the President's Men* was automatically given an R rating because its dialogue contained a familiar four-letter word. At the appeal hearing, the head of the Code and Rating Administration, historian Richard Heffner, himself argued in favor of a PG rating for the film, on the grounds that one word ought not to keep young people from seeing a well-made and important dramatization of political history.

Norman . . . Is That You?, a lightweight situation comedy done television-style on

A relatively chaste love scene between Sarah Miles and Christopher Jones in Ryan's Daughter, *first earned the film a Restricted rating, softened under protest to a PG.*

tape, was also rated R in 1976 because it deals with a father's discovery that his son is homosexual. MGM appealed successfully and *Norman* was re-rated PG.

The ratings have also been attacked as a form of prior censorship, in that the filmmaker is told after a review of his script what will have to come out if he hopes to receive

Movies of quality continued to find audiences, as did Lion in Winter, *superbly acted by Katharine Hepburn and Peter O'Toole.*

a G rating or a PG or an R. Since financing for a movie these days is sometimes contingent on preserving a particular rating, the filmmaker is not invariably free to accept whatever rating the Code Administration predicts he will get on the completed film. There have also been cries that Valenti ratings open "floodgates of filth," although such shrill alarums usually indiscriminately refer to the skin-flicks, which are made and distributed outside the mainstream movie system and have no links at all with the ratings.

Yet the fact is that the filmmaker can presently say, do, show, and treat on the screen virtually anything that is even remotely of interest to a particular audience. The cost may be an X or R rating, but if the "cost" can be paid, the freedom of expression is there.

Compared with the nit-picking precision of the old Code, the present system is uncommonly flexible within fairly general guidelines. In a society whose tolerances continue to change, the flexibility is necessary and helpful, even if there are times the filmmaker finds the vagueness of the guidelines as bothersome as the specifics used to be.

It seems abundantly clear that the process of historical change, which reached a peak late in 1968, has left significant marks on a great majority of the movies made since then, and not only on those movies that make either legitimate or exploitive use of sexual themes or of violence.

Of the major films released in 1968, *Oliver!* was one of few that would have been done in exactly the same way if it had been made five years before, or five years later. But *Funny Girl*, *The Lion in Winter*, *Isadora*, *The Producers*, and *Rachel, Rachel* all told us more and gave us wider insights into the multiple conditions of man.

It remained for *Midnight Cowboy* in 1969 to become the first X-rated film to be named Best Picture by the Motion Picture Academy.

But *Midnight Cowboy* is not simply a master-work of the film form; it also is the first graphic evidence of what genuine freedom can mean to a dedicated filmmaker such as John Schlesinger.

The materials on first sight are scabrous. A semiliterate idler (Jon Voigt) comes from Texas to New York City to make his way in the world as a stud hustler, a homosexual prostitute. He drifts into palship with Ratso Rizzo (Dustin Hoffman), a tubercular grifter who talks a confident game but gets along by rifling pay phones for left coins. The stud's misadventures are briefly, raucously funny but his life is a quick descent to the cold and gritty lower depths of the urban slums—hell in a condemned and abandoned tenement. In the end, fleeing what could well be arrest on a murder charge, the hustler and his sick pal ride the bus through the bright sunlight of Miami. But for Ratso the sunshine has come too late; he has just died.

The performances by Voigt and Hoffman were superlatively detailed. The critics (and, later, the church groups that keep an eye on the movies) were quick to see that beneath its strident and seamy surfaces *Midnight Cowboy* was both a morality play and a deeply spiritual document. The script, superbly written by Waldo Salt, attested to the possibility that love and compassion could exist in even the most desperate of human conditions, and that under provocation it could as well be man's better instincts, an inherent self-sacrificing fineness, that come to the fore.

The movie used the new latitudes of the medium to deal accurately and credibly with a sordid slice of contemporary life. The triumph of the film was to place a moment of time in the presumed context of all time. Its comparison, no less than its candor, made *Midnight Cowboy* an enduring piece of art, a milestone for the new era to come.

Reflecting the new day in film, John Schlesinger's Midnight Cowboy, *Jon Voigt as a stud hustler, was the first X-rated Oscar winner.*

Visions of violence

Conflict plus action equals violence. The movies seized upon the equation from the start and have never let go. The very first footages may have been glimpses, astonishing because they moved, of the ordinary world—waves breaking, a train puffing into a railway station—but Edwin S. Porter's *The Great Train Robbery* in 1903, with its final image of a six-shooter firing point-blank at the camera, is the more enduring, symbolic beginning.

Since then, men, women, and children of every race, creed, and previous condition of servitude have by the tens of thousands been shot down and blown up, whumped, stomped, trampled, sawed, fractured, punctured, bruised, defenestrated, whipped, strangled, scalped, scalded, snake bit, poisoned, burned; thrown from cars, trains, planes, and boats; booby-trapped, crushed, stabbed, impaled; struck with darts, arrows, spears, and daggers; slashed with swords; also smothered, fried, cannibalized, and scared to death.

The curious and revealing fact is that so little outcry over all this bloodletting was heard until comparatively recent years. There have always been those who feared and despised nearly everything the movies did, and who included film violence in the long litany of their discontents. But the ground swells of Middle-American agitation that led in the 1930s to the Legion of Decency and the Hays Code were caused mainly by matters of sex, not significantly by matters of violence.

In relative terms, not much has changed. Movies are busted for sex, not violence. The struggles to come up with an appeal-proof definition of what constitutes obscenity have not to my knowledge embraced the idea that violence can be obscene. The censorship bills in the legislatures and the ballot initiatives (such as California's Proposition 18 a few years ago) are very precise about what is not nice—sexually. Only recently did the industry's Code and Rating Administration for the first time

Characteristic social violence of the late 1960s ripped through films like Strawberry Statement, *with its climactic campus protest and riot.*

give a film an X solely because of its violence
—for an imported martial arts epic called
The Street Fighter. The city of Chicago in
1976 passed an ordinance making screen brutality actionable in law. The ordinance was
urged into being by Mayor Richard Daley,
and his rising impatience with violence may
well bespeak a larger restlessness with gratuitous gore.

But if even now in the mid-1970s American
society is still more uptight about sex than
about violence, there nevertheless have been
profound changes—in the nature of film violence and in the concern over what it may
be doing to us.

It is now clear that the opening up of the
American screen in the 1960s, the casting off
of reticences that had been imposed by the
Code, the courts, and not least by a kind of
unwritten consensus on what was acceptable,
affected not only language, themes, nudity,
and sexual conduct, but also violence.

It was not just that we watched blood spurt
from a fresh-cut throat in Sam Peckinpah's
The Wild Bunch, or saw Bonnie and Clyde
fall dying in a storm of bullets in the slow-mo-
tion ballet, so poetic, so graphic, and so horrifying, that ended Arthur Penn's film. It was
that a whole convention of violence by which
the movies had lived and died for decades had
been overturned.

The nice, comforting distinction between
violence as an element of storytelling and violence as a fact of life was blurred. It was all
still make-believe, of course, clever artifice,
but there was suddenly a new handling of violence that no longer allowed us to ignore the
implications or the real-life resonances of
what we watched. In his celebrated and courageous change of mind about the merits of
Bonnie and Clyde, film critic Joseph Morgenstern of *Newsweek* said that the movie showed
that killing kills. Yes, and that gunshot
wounds are ugly and painful, even agonizing,
and that death is not a sweet and easeful sleep

The new graphics of violence made Sam Peckinpah's
The Wild Bunch, *with William Holden, a very
bloody landmark for its concluding orgy of killing.*

90

A woman on the attack, for a change, Jane Fonda flails at Donald Sutherland in Klute.

but a permanent state, often gruesomely arrived at.

All movie violence was never created equal. The wasteful irony of death by war was eloquently demonstrated in *All Quiet on the Western Front* nearly a half-century ago. Yet the overwhelming use of violence then and, less overwhelmingly, now was diversionary. And the compact between screen and viewer was that it was all good, gory fun—or maybe good, gory drama—whose reverberations were guaranteed not to last much beyond the foyer on the way to the street. Gangsters strewn around the hooch-filled warehouse or gunslingers crumpled in the dust outside the false-front Long Branch saloon would arise and dust themselves off and proceed to the commissary for chicken-salad sandwiches, and it was a comfort to think of it that way. It was drama as catharsis because it could be passed off so easily.

At that, the prevalence of violence in the movies was greater from the 1930s forward than it might have been because the Hays Code, taking effect in 1934, set such sharp restrictions on the themes movies could handle and introduced such puritanical inhibitions into the visible relations between men and women. Even couples established as respectably married could not be shown sharing a double bed. Necessity mothered some admirable film gifts for innuendo and metaphor (waves breaking rhythmically over warm rocks) as ways of dealing with steamy emotions. But all those negative steamy emotions—hatred, revenge, murderous jealousy— were easier to deal with. Violence took on the additional function of a surrogate for sex, in a way that distorted the frequency and consequences of both activities in real life.

What effect all the mayhem had on the collective consciousness of those of us who grew up with it is not certain and probably never will be. If the Code induced violence as an alternative to sex, it did also insist that crime and violence could not be glorified, justified, or condoned; and violent crime was always punished in the end, by fate if not by law. Nobody got away with anything, no matter how badly story logic and common sense had to be abused to achieve the required retribution in the last reel.

A Beverly Hills psychiatrist, writing in the Los Angeles *Times* a few years ago, said that the real danger of the excessive use of violence in films and on television was the reiterated, implied message that only violence solves problems. It was not that it looked like fun; it was that there were no other choices.

A woman under attack, Karen Black fights off the outrage of rape in Jack Nicholson's look at a decaying society, Drive, He Said.

Yet no one really told us that in the 1930s and 1940s, when you knew the violence was actually nonviolent, and the good guys won anyway. The worry about violence grew more real as the quality and kind of mayhem grew more intense.

The old Code limped to a dusty and unlamented death in 1968, after thirty-four years of mischief and worse. (Fritz Lang tells a story, one among hundreds, of an encounter he had with the Breen Office over the script of *House on the River* in 1950. It called for Louis Hayward, realizing he had strangled a woman, to cry 'My God!' Impossible, said the Office; the man, being a murderer, was not entitled to invoke the name of God. Well, Lang inquired wickedly, did the Office have a suggestion as to what the character *could* say in the circumstances. "Good Heavens!?" asked the Office, helpfully.)

The new, or Valenti, era makes possible a violence more horrendously explicit than ever before. The special-effects lads keep outdoing themselves in a way to make Grand Guignol green with envy. Brain matter plays against a wall, gouts of blood leap from every wound, the chain saw munches hungrily into bone and sinew, the blood-dripping innards fall toward the laps of the audience through the miracle of 3D. Yet most of these usages of violence are merely old ketchup spiced up. They are not departures from but extensions of the long-standing idea of violence understood to be make-believe and nonviolent. It is gratuitous and bloody awful, but it bears the same relation to reality as Mickey Mouse does to rat-infested tenements.

The more interesting changes in the use of violence are really less evident. Most important—and in the most controversial of the films of violence—it has become not a device but a theme.

Bonnie and Clyde (1967) was about several things, but one of them was violence as an inevitable product of economic distress. Arthur Penn and producer-star Warren Beatty were conscious of the parallels between the Depression of the thirties and the ghetto violence of the sixties. The way Bonnie and Clyde became mythic, romantic heroes because of their attacks on the economic establishment—the foreclosing banks—was also what the movie was about. The bullet-ridden ballet that carried them to legend was an inspired manipulation of violence, preserving through the languid slow motion the sense of their romanticism but also confronting us interminably with the ugly fact of the slaughter. It was impossible, as Joseph Morgenstern has said, to escape the fact that killing kills.

The Wild Bunch (1969) remains, I think, both the most graphic and extensive and the most argued-over of the violent films *about* violence. Peckinpah established his dark point of view—that man has not only a capacity for violence but a taste for it—from the start, with a scene of children torturing insects, and kept up the slaughter until it was impossible to leave the theater feeling anything but numbed and drained. (*The Wild Bunch* may be the most convincing argument for the Aristotelian theory of catharsis in modern times.)

Peckinpah, who is both deeply cynical and bottomlessly sentimental, doubtless had it both ways, exploiting the violence even as he and it confirmed his point that we exult in

Shooting their way into history, Beatty and Dunaway were romanticized folk heroes in Arthur Penn's Bonnie and Clyde, *but the film made clear that violence is ugly and killing kills.*

it. To disagree with him was to despise the film as a statement, however much one admired his remorseless skill. But there could be no doubt that he was dealing with violence and commenting on it from a position that has been consistent through his work.

In *Straw Dogs* (1971) Peckinpah also used fully the new freedom in depicting varieties of violence, and its emotional power was the greater because the story was set in a credible present rather than in a storied Old West. The simple-minded messages, of violence as a rite of passage to manhood, of rape as something women really like if they'll only admit it, were harder to take than his well-founded suspicion of the latent violence in us all that he advanced in *The Wild Bunch*.

If the opening up of the screen was a removing of restraints long in place, it was also a removing of comfortable certainty. The old confidence that virtue would triumph (or do no worse than break even) and evil be punished went the way of premarital virginity and much else. It is no longer sure that the good guy will win: in the wake of *Easy Rider* (1969), you could be equally sure he would lose. Indeed, the last sequence of *Easy Rider,* with Peter Fonda and Dennis Hopper blasted into

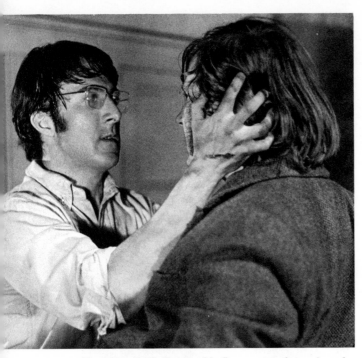

Forced to kill, Dustin Hoffman attacks an invader and becomes a man in the arguable logic of Sam Peckinpah's Straw Dogs.

eternity, as if on a whimsical impulse, by a chortling and anonymous redneck aboard a pickup truck, is as perfectly symbolic of the new violence as Edwin Porter's trick shot was of the founding impulse to violence sixty-some years earlier.

The old violence had, in a sense, fought fair. If the villain/bully/bad guy got in his licks early on, you knew he would in turn get what was coming to him (and more besides) before the picture's end. If the viewer's stomach knotted in helpless rage at watching the bound victim beaten, it would unknot when justice was finally served.

But what if justice isn't served—and you can no longer be sure it will be. It is not possible any more to sit back confident that the violence is make-believe, comfortingly unreal. Artifice it certainly is, but so harsh and sobering a reflection of the real world as makes no

difference. And when injustice and evil go unchallenged, as they did in the murders of all three protagonists in *Easy Rider,* the viewer carries the furies of frustration with him—and the messages—for a long time after.

The messages of *Easy Rider* seemed to me to be both multiple and muffled. One certainty was that a lethal intolerance existed along the gaps of generation and life style in the United States in the 1960s. But another was that you can't be free and easy, can't opt out of all social responsibility. It is the message of intolerance that survives.

Disasters are a kind of violence and just now disasters are big box office. The two biggest of the disaster epics, *The Towering Inferno* and *Earthquake* (both 1974), have become controversial in curious ways. Writers who do not usually deal with movies have attacked *Inferno* because its images of people burning to death are so literal and convincing. "I don't want to go to the movies to see people fry," one of them said not long ago. *Earthquake,* to a lesser extent, has also been attacked for making catastrophe so believable.

The stir over these movies seems excessive. They proclaim from the start their intentions of being super-colossal, star-studded, high-budget, glossy entertainments in a very special Hollywood tradition. And *Earthquake* in particular, with its continuing comic cameo by Walter Matthau, is at considerable pains to reassure us that the pains are make-believe.

The wizardry of the special effects in both films must delight any film buff as an end in itself. And indeed, whatever you see on the screen in those films is less affecting than the uncomfortable powers of implication the films have. If you live in earthquake country you cannot escape the memory of those queasy, terrifying moments when nothing stood still. Imagination builds steeper horrors than Universal Studios can. The worry of *Towering Inferno* (beyond the claustrophobia)

The gory excitements of violent disaster made Irwin Allen's Towering Inferno *and other multiple jeopardy films into towering hits.*

96

is that in a real fire Steve McQueen and Paul Newman would not be around to lend a valiant hand. The qualms will not stay behind in the foyer: that is the problem.

Violence sells, but it is far from clear that all violence does sell. The superactive blacksploitation films and the kung fu epics (whose novelty is wearing off if it hasn't done so already) meld violence to other elements. And there is at least some evidence that gratuitous violence does not really sit well with the audiences. *The Hunting Party* (1971), for example, in which a vengeful Gene Hackman, armed with an extremely powerful rifle, picks off one by one from a great distance the men he imagines have kidnapped his wife, was a commercial disaster. Violence visited on those unable to defend themselves (the bound, the sleeping, those—as here—too distant to see the enemy) is, I've always felt, the hardest for audiences to cope with. It was probably for that reason *The Hunting Party* failed. It was not about violence or much of anything else: it was an exercise in plot leading to a sour ending.

The whole sense of the movies in the last several years is of muscles newly found, of capacities for both power and delicacy newly unlimbered. You feel, in a film like *Report to the Commissioner* (1975), a new freedom to convey the whole violence of life, of which the guns and the beatings are only part. There are the violences to truth and justice, the rankling brutalities of the street, the subtle assaults of corruption. But *Report to the Commissioner* failed as well, most probably because its story was so grimly pessimistic.

What might be potentially dangerous in a new day is that the movies need no longer even their scales. Justice, which once needed to be seen to be done, can now be seen to be undone. The good guys are winning a little more than they did for a while, even if they are the questionably good guys of *The Sting.*

The horrors of war, seen on Liv Ullmann's face, was the vivid message of Ingmar Bergman's grimly surrealistic Shame *in 1968.*

98

But the new freedom is also a freedom to arouse and enrage, and leave it all hanging out.

One of the highest-grossing films of 1974 was Michael Winner's *Death Wish*, in which Charles Bronson becomes a one-man vigilante gang, taking the law into his own hands and killing muggers in cold blood (or hot blood) to avenge the murder of his wife and the maiming of his daughter. Entrapping his victims and outwitting the ineffectual and hobbled policeman, the Bronson character played to the really deep-seated fears and resentments of the audience and exploited them in a way that seemed as despicable as the film's success was predictable.

Yet the new openness and diversity of the screen seems, whatever its possibilities for mischief, far less dangerous and oppressive than the monolithic tidiness of the old Code days, with its imposed moralities, its mandatory punishings, and its single-minded view of the way the world must be.

Film now offers no single view of violence or anything else. Each movie sets its attitudes afresh each time, hinting as early as the titles how hard its make-believe will work to make us believe. Within the diversity, there is room for the violence of disbelief along with the violence all too credibly rooted in life.

It is possible to grow desperately weary of the acting-out of man's inhumanity to man, and I have the feeling that the filmmakers (and the television-makers) are feeding an appetite that is very near to being sated. *Missouri Breaks* emerged in mid-1976 to loud fanfares, with Jack Nicholson and Marlon Brando co-starring and the respected Arthur Penn directing. There was much to be said against it, not least the fact that art was an afterthought in what took shape as a totally commercial project everyone did just for the money. Against its odds, it had some amusing moments, but its savagery was uncommonly

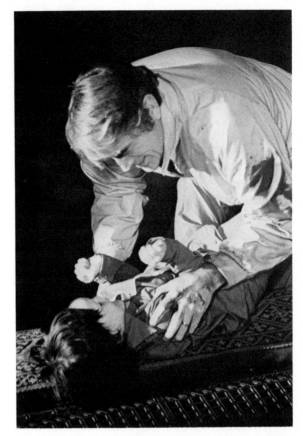

Ritual violence, as Gregory Peck's killing of his possessed son, made The Omen *as much of an occult success as* The Exorcist *was a few years ago.*

graphic and nasty. (Brando's favorite death weapon was the grappling hook thrown to hit right between the eyes.) The movie flopped for several reasons, but I incline to think that the ugliness of the violence was chief among them.

Like *The Exorcist* (1973) before it, *The Omen* was one of 1976's slickest and largest-grossing films (although an English critic neatly described it as second-rite). Its brutality, including an impaling, and the murder of a demonic child, was shocking and specific, but whether the violence as such was the movie's lure is unclear and doubtful. Like *The Exorcist*, *The Omen* suggested that higher

Taking the law in his own hands, Charles Bronson avenged his wife's murder in Death Wish, *which played on the audiences' fears of street violence.*

101

powers of both good and evil are out there somewhere, fighting furiously with us mortals as their pawns, and it is nice to think that there is anything beyond our mean streets.

Two more of the big 1976 films were crucially violent: Martin Scorsese's *Taxi Driver* and John Schlesinger's *Marathon Man*. Until it reached its muddled ending, when you felt that Scorsese and the writer, Paul Schrader, could not agree on the meaning of what had gone before on *their* mean streets, *Taxi Driver* was both a grueling and all-too-believable examination of a disturbed and not-too-bright loner being driven to mass murder by the sordid, impersonal, degrading vileness of a city's lower depths. Its last bloodbath was horrifying, revolting, but the violence came as a strange kind of relief. (Robert DeNiro as the killer chose an unexpected set of victims—who were themselves unsympathetic and villainous.) Whether the bloody violence was in itself the film's attraction is again unclear. Part of the success is unquestionably due to the large following both Scorsese and DeNiro have among steady filmgoers. Another element, surely, is that Scorsese and Schrader spoke with passion and believability about much that is wanting in big city life, and some in the audience sensed the filmmakers shared their rage and spoke for them.

Marathon Man was something else again, a superbly executed but essentially traditional genre film, a violent thriller with less on its mind than, say, *Chinatown* (from the same producer, Robert Evans). Its violence was so graphic as to induce revulsion rather than excitement; like *Bonnie and Clyde*, it left no doubt that maiming hurts and death is gray-green and final. In the longer run, it may well prove that the accuracy of the violence worked against rather than for the film's success and that if *Marathon Man* is ultimately a large money-maker it will be because of the intricacies and mystifications of the plot and

A fare to remember, Martin Scorsese rides to kill his wife's lover as psychotic cabbie Robert De Niro watches in Scorsese's Taxi Driver.

the excellence of the star acting (by Dustin Hoffman and Laurence Olivier and a large supporting cast).

For the rest of it, the appeal of the exploitively super-violent black and martial arts films has now unmistakably waned. Spectacular action, not necessarily the same thing as person-to-person violence, has its audiences, as in the mini-vogue of car chase films, like the high-grossing *Gone in 60 Seconds*. What begins to seem true is that filmgoers can take the sight of personal suffering or leave it alone, and that the coming reaction against violence may itself be violent.

Marriage and other disasters

"They lived happily ever after," so the movies said, tiptoeing away from the bedroom door. They said it for sixty years. Now, for the last ten years, the movies have been proving that the couple will be lucky if they get through the weekend together.

Once the idealized and optimistic presumptions about life according to the Hays Code were no longer enforceable, the movies changed many of their tunes. The good guys were no longer sure to win, the bad guys were no longer certain to lose. Crime looked suspiciously glorious now and again, and it sometimes paid. You could no longer be sure about anything.

The most sustained and even savage turnabout in movie attitudes has been toward marriage. In one decade marriage was the end of all earthly cares; in the next it was the start of all earthly troubles. Almost overnight the institution went from sunset panacea (the couple silhouetted, gazing into radiant clouds, nothing ahead but tranquility and forever-

ness) to gray dawn in no man's land and another day in the wars of marital attrition.

Of course, bad marriages were a staple of comedy from the silent-movie days forward, and henpecked husbands and their muscular, shrewish wives were opposing sides in the slapstick mix-ups that never ended. When Laurel and Hardy were not mangling a new scheme to get rich quick, they were calculating how to maneuver a little free time away from their justifiably mistrusting wives. W. C. Fields made misogyny a part of his comedic character. He was a constant loser in the homefront battles, generally under attack from both a shrill wife and an even shriller mother-in-law.

Yet even in comedies there was no real quarrel with the institution of marriage, only with its temporary inhabitants. Usually in feature films—if not always in short subjects, where there wasn't time—a lovey-dovey peace was restored by the final reel, often with husbands unexpectedly triumphant and wives submissive and repentant—at least for the mo-

Doubtful models for marital bliss, W. C. Fields and Alison Skipworth played at togetherness in several 1930s films.

104

ment. Full of splendors, Fields's *The Bank Dick* (1941) is, among other things, a heartwarming display of the harassed husband's harrumphing turnabout from victim to victor.

There were serious films as well that acknowledged marriages could go awry. Few are more moving than William Wyler's *Dodsworth*, produced by Sam Goldwyn in 1936 from the Sinclair Lewis novel about a middle-aged man trying to keep alive his marriage to a bored and selfish wife. It was not a commercial success, a fact that may help explain why the movies so seldom dealt seriously with marriage, and so regularly walked away from it just as the wedding bells pealed, as if there were nothing more to be said.

The movies of an earlier time have a lot to answer for, because they veiled the married state in a fashion that almost totally disguised its real nature, its real rewards, and its all-too-real perils. Under the Code the movies could not in any meaningful way consider the physical side of marriage. By inference wedlock seemed a quite curious, upright, and eunuchoidal state, but one that also was understood to be a sort of infinitely desirable magical mystery tour of heaven. It was not that the movies should have been serving as visual marriage manuals; it was that their suggestive powers were so mischievously misleading—singing of honeymoons and ignoring thereafters, equating partner-picking with beauty contests.

When things changed they changed drastically, overcompensating for all the oversimple things the movies had been saying about matrimony all those years.

Who's Afraid of Virginia Woolf? from 1966 is as much a film landmark in attitudes toward marriage as in its candor, openness, and language (see Chapter 6). In it, the comedy of bickering becomes the tragedy of invective. There are two marriages on view, each marked by fear, failure, and disappointment, the core

Lovely couple Albert Finney and Audrey Hepburn were Two for the Road, *hitting all of the pot-holes of modern marriage in Stanley Donen's sleek film from a Frederic Raphael script.*

of love in each relationship buried or denied (because to confess love is to confess need, and to admit need is to surrender some last shield against the world). *Virginia Woolf* is an extreme and perverse statement on marriage as a fiery matrix, but it is a tonic and

useful alternative to the insipid romantic view of marriage expressed as a state in which to live happily ever after.

From the 1960s onward, the movies began to depict marriage as the testing, complicated, troubled, and changing relationship it is.

The year 1967 was really a significant one because the first movies reflecting the somewhat liberalized Code were coming along. By the peculiar lumpings that sometimes occur in movie content, three lighthearted but re-

vealing examinations of modern marriage were released that year.

The best of them was Stanley Donen's *Two for the Road,* from an ingenious original script by English novelist Frederic Raphael, which moved in and out among several slices of time in the characters' lives. The stars were Audrey Hepburn and Albert Finney, whose relationship began as a premarital affair. Later, as their marriage eroded, each of them had an extramarital affair, although these led not to

His marriage with Debbie Reynolds failing, both loneliness and poverty loomed for Dick Van Dyke in Divorce—American Style.

the end of the marriage but to forgiveness and a fresh affirmation of the rightness of the married state. The tone of the movie was romantic and escapist, the stars intensely glamorous even though their language and behavior were untraditional. The movie also was filled with insightful observations about marriage: the dangerously distractive effect of a man's work, the resentments and jealousies a first child can produce, the indifference, irrationality, and even contempt marital familiarity can breed.

It may be easier (certainly it is more colorful) to restore marriage in a sports car speeding to the French Riviera than in a station wagon on the way to the supermarket. What made *Two for the Road* impressive was that amidst its glossy surroundings there was the

recognition of familiar back-home problems. The upbeat ending (guardedly, rather than totally, optimistic) carried weight because Finney and Hepburn were credible people, however romantic their surroundings. Finney in particular spent much of his time being mulish, even downright unattractive, but he was saved for us, as for Hepburn, by his final, rumpled charm.

For those who have gone the divorce route, the Bud Yorkin–Norman Lear *Divorce American Style* (directed by Yorkin, scripted by Lear from a story by Bob Kaufman) was

Divorce from Sophia Loren is absolutely impossible for Marcello Mastroianni, who had been tricked into marrying her in the first place, in Vittorio De Sica's Marriage—Italian Style.

not a comedy but a tragedy in the thinnest of disguises. It rang with fury at all the mechanisms of divorce (not the institution but the process) and employed comedy to make its passionate statements about insidious friends, indifferent lawyers, ineffectual counselors, and inequitable financial settlements. In the movie's finest moment, several couples converge on one house to exercise visitation rights on all the children of all the permutations of their marriages. A whole convoy of reloaded station wagons guns off into the afternoon, leaving one small, overlooked child all by herself in the middle of the lawn.

The point of view was male: Dick Van Dyke reduced from affluent executive to pauper by the settlement, Jason Robards plotting desperately to get ex-wife Jean Simmons remarried so he can live again. The jokes were overstated and bitter, but they were still more convincing than the ending, which reunited Van Dyke and Debbie Reynolds, the whole exercise having been a dreadful mistake. The sardonic detailing of their marital past did not invite optimism about a brighter tomorrow.

A Guide for the Married Man, the least successful of the three films, tried the comic touch to make philandery the all-American game. There were some fine sketchy jokes as

Elliott and Natalie and Robert and Dyan (Gould, Wood, Culp, Cannon) stayed both unswapped and unhappy in that semi-daring 1960s comedy about marriage, Bob and Carol and Ted and Alice.

110

Walter Matthau led Robert Morse, and vice versa, on a tour of attempted seductions. (Gene Kelly directed, from a script by Frank Tarloff.) The trouble was that a little truth was worse than none, and the basic assumption of the movies that sex is a male game and women the movable pawns seemed so well validated by the American experience that the jokes rang hollow. Cheating seen as a source of innocent merriment—like bowling or pinochle—refused to stay innocent or merry. Matthau went home, unsullied, to an Inger Stevens so warmly womanly as to make an instant mockery of her husband's farcical chasing about. Its ending merely confirmed the movie's intent to tease rather than deal, even comedically, with some hard and unattractive truths about what had not yet begun to be called male chauvinism.

Mate-swapping was considered in *Bob and Carol and Ted and Alice* (1969). The two couples of the movie's title examine all the possibilities and at the last possible minute reject them. They retreat from sinful Las Vegas to their safe Los Angeles homes, relieved but unhappy, or maybe it is unrelieved but happy. Seen in retrospect, the Mike Frankovich movie, written by Larry Tucker and Paul Mazursky and directed by Mazursky, seems as indecisive as the couples themselves, torn between an old orthodoxy and a new permissiveness, acknowledging mate-swapping as a new social phenomenon but not really examining the peculiar restlessness of which it was, or is, only a symptom. Still, the movie acknowledged the phenomenon. It did leave an uneasiness, a sense that its ending was an adjournment rather than a dismissal.

Loving, early in 1970, was a lovely, lost movie, flawed by a showy and farcical ending, that in its earlier reels had a lot to say about middle-class, early-middle-age love and marriage. George Segal played a competent commercial artist commuting from Connecticut

A counterview of happy marriage, Loving, *had a man (George Segal) commuting between his wife and his mistress and about to lose them both.*

to Manhattan and from wife Eva Marie Saint to a young mistress who, however, finds a better keepsake. Like *Divorce American Style,* *Loving* offered an all-revealing and unforgettable moment. Diana Douglas, in the process of divorce, shows her house to Segal and Saint and, near bitter tears, describes the warmth and gaiety that once filled the place. Even by 1970 the Segal character—frustrated creatively, weary of the rat race, haunted by fears of declining sexual power and attractiveness, feeling not so much out of love as out of time —was indeed becoming a familiar screen figure. Segal has made this type of character even more familiar since then. In *Loving,* he appeared finally to have lost, to have permanently locked himself out in the cold.

Brenda Vaccaro ate her way out of a very thin, bad marriage (unintentionally but luckily) in the film I Love My Wife.

It grows more difficult to separate the movies' changed perceptions of marriage from their changing perceptions of women. Even when movies about marriage are nominally from the man's point of view, it is the woman's attitudes that determine the course of events. They may be reacting, as before, to situations that were not of their making, but they are reacting with a new independence and new expectations about their role.

I Love My Wife (1970) centered on Elliott Gould as a doctor who becomes a swinger of obsessive and destructive determination. The rough-textured script (by the same Bob Kaufman whose story was the basis of *Divorce American Style*) insists that the character is what the society made him, and it may be. Brenda Vaccaro is the loving wife who sustains him through medical school, bears him children, and lets herself go blimp fat and sloppy. She tosses him out, gets herself back in shape, and begins to remake a better life for herself. Gould, as we leave him, is at a bar, about to pick up a stewardess, hating himself for being so successful at it but unable to stop. He is a sad and unattractive figure, and whether or not he indicts the society for being uptight about sex, the promise of the movie is that his wife will be all right and he won't.

In the Mel Frank–Jack Rose romantic comedy *A Touch of Class* (1973), George Segal again plays the protagonist, engineering a love affair with Glenda Jackson in the face of innumerable comic obstacles. Segal's wife, seen only at a distance, is remote, rich, cool, well organized, and less than a barrel of laughs, while Jackson is successful, independent, strong-willed, free-spirited, and spontaneous. In the end, although it appears obvious that she and Segal have fallen in love, Jackson breaks off the affair. There has been a specific misunderstanding, but it is clear that the trouble is larger than that. Their commitments are seen to be unequal. Asking nothing more than love, Jackson is still consigned to a kind of inferior, waiting status that is at odds with the rest of her life. She strides off in the Soho rain to find a taxi; Segal, arriving too late, watches her go. She, you have the feeling, will do better next time; he may well not. She invites our sympathy; he settles for our pity. A marriage has been preserved, but in this movie era it looks less like a triumph of good

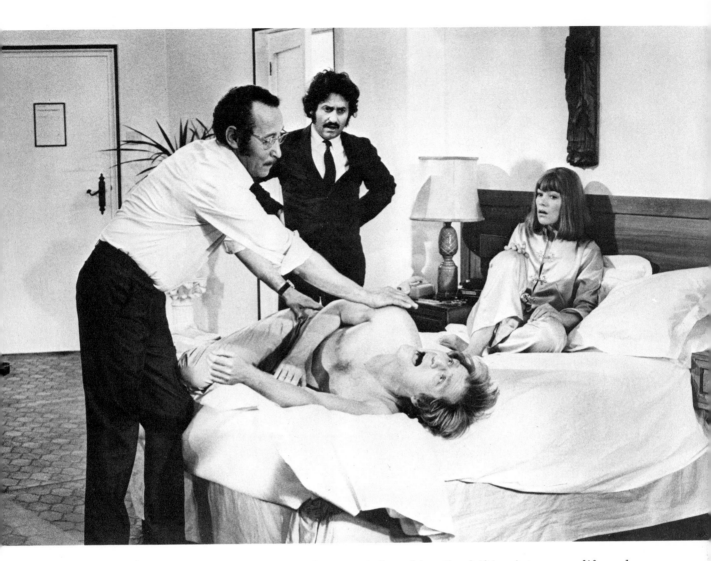

Crying out, George Segal as a married buyer with a bad back got little sympathy from Glenda Jackson, the mistress who won all the sympathy in the comedy A Touch of Class.

thinking than a concession to convenience and possibly a surrender to the security of the wife's wealth.

Segal, yet again, in Paul Mazursky's *Blume in Love* (1973), loves his wife but loses her when she finds him making love to his secretary. The movie is his, and yet it eventually feels as though it is dominated by Susan An-

spach, as his wife, drifting into a new life and a new romance (with Kris Kristofferson). Segal does his own drifting, into an affair with an old friend (Marsha Mason). Still, he loves his wife, shadows her, invades her house, rapes her . . . and wins her back. Seldom in recent years has a movie tried so hard to say something sentimental and traditional with such unconvincing results. Segal's wife has been so justifiably offended and repelled by him that it is never clear why she consents to have him back or why, in fact, he wants to face her hostility. He seems doubly a fool to forego the warmth and understanding of the relationship with Marsha Mason. Mazursky made a statement that was a reaffirmation of marriage (positive in the sense that the return in *A Touch of Class* was not), and this film marked a turnaround in the marriage movies. The popularity of *Blume* may have owed as much to the singularity of its message as to the charm of its players and the skill of its comedy.

Stewart Stern, who had written the script of *Rachel, Rachel* for Joanne Woodward, wrote an original screenplay for her in *Summer Wishes, Winter Dreams* (1973). As the spoiled, bored, self-centered wife of a successful Manhattan ophthalmologist (played with marvelous restraint and sensitivity by Martin Balsam), she is at the crisis point in middle age, forced to confront the disappointments of a life whose end is no longer unthinkably remote. Her dilemma is equal to that of her male counterparts in comparable films with a male point of view. The wishes and dreams are beyond hoping, and the swift death of her mother forces the cruel truth home. Her son, a homosexual, has renounced the family and is living in Europe; her daughter is outspokenly unsympathetic to Woodward.

Balsam takes his wife abroad on a tour that includes a visit to Bastogne, where he had fought in the brutal winter of 1944. His soliloquy, remembering how it was, is a strongly affecting piece of acting. Little enough happens thereafter, except that the moment has jolted his wife out of her self-absorption and into a renewed awareness of their need for each other. The ending is not a reconciliation but a resignation, an acceptance that their lives are now too linked ever to be separated. As an affirmation of marriage it is different from the other films in that it is positive and believable, and gives a reassuring endorsement of the institution.

Last Tango in Paris (1973) will probably not be remembered as having had much of anything to do with marriage, but the notoriety of its love scenes ought not to obscure the fact that Brando was walking the streets of Paris red-eyed, unshaven, and zombielike because his wife had just committed suicide. In his rootless and unloving life, she was evidently the first, and one of the few, to give him any sense of stability and place; and although they had their troubles, his love and need for her were manifest and intense. His despair over what seemed to him her betrayal and abandonment, in his raging soliloquy amidst the candles and flowers at her catafalque, makes a scene of very great power, so anguished as to seem an invasion of privacy. The death of love and marriage has not often been conveyed in terms at once so unsentimental and tragic.

Produced originally as six one-hour episodes for Scandinavian television, Ingmar Bergman's *Scenes from a Marriage* (1974), re-edited by Bergman himself into a three-hour film, is unquestionably the calmest, most penetrating, and most universal look at middle-class marriage we have yet had. There are long moments when Bergman seems to have been eavesdropping on us all, although, having been married five times himself, he doubtless had need to listen to anything but his own memory.

His couple (Liv Ullmann and Erland Josephson) are smugly content: she is a prosperous divorce lawyer, he a social scientist. But at a morose and drunken dinner party there is another couple whose gut-spilling hatred of each other prefigures the troubles Ullman and Josephson will shortly be having. He falls in love with a younger woman (we never see her but are given to understand that she is oversexed, underbrained, and all too soon a bore). The wife, momentarily stunned, pulls herself back together and comes to realize that for all her achievements she has really spent her life becoming what others (notably her father and her husband) wanted her to be. If she

Marriage Swedish style looked no happier there than elsewhere in the world in Ingmar Bergman's Scenes From a Marriage, *starring Liv Ullmann and Erland Josephson, here briefly tender.*

114

gains in assurance and strength, Josephson goes a bit seedy. There are disappointments in his career and financial pinches; he drinks rather more than he should. Each marries again, securely but presumably not contentedly. In a postlude twenty years after they first married, Bergman has the couple meeting again as afternoon lovers in hotels and, finally, in a country cabin where, in the middle of a cold night, they cling to each other like children, consoling each other. One does not sense that they will remarry; it seems too late and too complicated for that. They have come to wisdom—late, perhaps, but their consolations can be seen as an affirmation. It is not the institution of marriage, Bergman seems to be saying, but the uses to which it has been placed that have gone awry. The movie was, in the cold night, oddly warming.

Shampoo (1975) was, in the warm Beverly Hills sunshine, a chilly, mordant look at modern relationships, including marriage and its terminal decay. Directed by Hal Ashby and written by Robert Towne (with heavy influence on both script and direction by producer-star Warren Beatty), *Shampoo* follows a fashionable hair stylist through several boudoirs' worth of overrich and underattended clients. The Beatty character is no Alfie: his is a complier rather than a seducer, a passive responder whose bed hopping keeps him from making any commitment. As subcultures go, the movie is both decorative and unattractive. The year is 1968, with the Nixon-Agnew election night occurring in midmovie. What links the sex and the politics is opportunism, a kind of operational chaos resulting from the absence of any long-range values still regarded as important and commanding. Without any confidence in love and permanent relationships (or any really deep-seated political convictions), the consequences are compromise, cynicism, and a despairing accommodation. Jeffersonian ideals have deteriorated into cover-ups at the highest levels of government, and romantic ideals have degenerated into an anarchic and uneasy permissiveness, unstable and unfulfilling, in our private lives.

Shampoo offers a quick tour of a world with no fixed values and no heroes or heroines in the traditional molds. It is a very narrow slice of life, confined in time and place, but no less accurate for its limited view. The film is full of insight into what might be called negative guidance, unsparing but not unsympathetic. *Carnal Knowledge* (1971) was more coldly clinical in its dissections of men, women, and marriage (see Chapter 9). *Shampoo* let us in on the pain as well as the numbness of its protagonists, reporting as forcefully as any film has been able to that the institution of marriage is in trouble.

(In the movies about tomorrow, marriage is not only in trouble, it has ceased to exist. This may be less a prediction than a matter of convenience for the filmmakers, who have

Future shocks in the film Logan's Run *included a brain-drain for Michael York and a world in which marriage was no more.*

other matters on their minds. But it true that the prophecies are of societies, like those in John Boorman's *Zardoz* from 1974 and Saul David's production of *Logan's Run* in 1976, where gratification is easy, continuous, and impersonal, and even relationships are as scarce as the common cold or pockets—no one requires pockets in the worlds of tomorrow. What is significant and reassuring is that the protagonists in *Zardoz, Logan's Run,* and many futurist fantasies yearn for relationships, if not for marriage, and the future never looks more bleak than in a lovelessness enforced as an act of big brotherly dogma.)

The troubles with marriage were not new. What was new in the late 1960s was the fidelity with which the movies could reflect infidelity and all other permutations on the intricate and baffling relationships between men and women. Despite the shifting attitudes toward marriage in the years since World War II, the institution probably changed less than the movies' ability to report upon it.

In the early 1970s, the movies' attitudes toward marriage began to reflect something more than their newfound powers of observation. The trend toward action and spectacle entailed a move away from tenderness and romance, in or out of marriage. Having learned to say that love dies, Hollywood (though not Europe) forgot how to say love lives, or chose not to on the grounds that the audience wanted other, larger excitements.

But ignoring the existence of strong and loving relationships is as distorting of the human condition as all those happy-ever-after fairy tales, and in the mid-1970s it seemed obvious that the movies would have to examine love and marriage yet again.

In *Dog Day Afternoon* (1975), drawn from an actual news story, Al Pacino was a bitterly perfect product of a society in which everything appeared to him to be permissible except love. Trapped in a whining and loveless heterosexual marriage, he was staging a tragicomic bank robbery to finance a sex-change operation for his new transvestite love. What gave the film a poignance, despite its circus ingredients, was a sense that the Pacino figure was not really unique in his despairing search for someone, anyone, to cling to.

And although its embrace of marriage was peculiarly motivated, Lina Wertmuller's

Sad-eyed in a sadder world, Giancarlo Giannini in Seven Beauties *chose marriage as the only refuge from an insane, collapsing world.*

Seven Beauties, an essay on survival amidst the horrors of World War II, ended with her hero, Giancarlo Giannini, gathering up the innocent girl—who has, like everyone else, been corrupted by the war—and sweeping her off into marriage (and child-bearing) as the only defense against the follies of the world.

The Wertmuller viewpoint is probably less an endorsement of marriage than a statement that the world is essentially anarchic, but it was still a reminder (to be noted for its rarity) that marriage has its points and its comforts.

Sylvester Stallone's marvelously upbeat and romantic *Rocky* (1976) ends with a freeze-frame as the battered hero (author Stallone himself) and his heroine (Talia Shire) embrace and say, "I love you," silhouetted not by the golden sunset but by the harsh lights of a fight arena. The moment is consciously and assertively old-fashioned. You have no doubt that marriage is in their future and that, *Rocky* being not least a fairy tale, they could well live happily ever after.

The movies in general are not apt to go back to their earlier uncritical visions of marriage, but having learned to report the dark side, the movies may now be able to tell the whole truth, seeing the institution for richer and for poorer, in health as well as in sickness.

Women and other objects

Traditionally, the movies have been one of society's foremost advocates of keeping women in their proper (that is, decidedly inferior) place. For every Madame Curie there have been 27,000 beautiful reactresses standing in the doorway waving goodbye and saying, with tears trickling down their stiff upper lips, "I'll wait for you, Fred, while you go off and do your noble thing."

Not that the movies haven't loved the ladies. Sixty years' worth of box-office-draw stars from Mary Pickford to Tatum O'Neal and Jodie Foster confirm that love. But for most of those years, the operative presumption has been that it is a man's world. And within that man's world, women are what things happen to, for, because of, or despite. Women endure things or watch things happen but even now it is rare for a film to have as its protagonist a woman who *makes* things happen; or for a film to present what *she* thinks, feels, or wants as its central concern; or to make its point of view *her* point of view.

By a not inconsiderable irony, women had more dignity back in the golden days of Hollywood when they were sex symbols rather than sex objects. They may have been out of the action, but they watched it, exquisitely groomed and gowned, from atop a pedestal reserved for symbols of great beauty, virtue, and desirability. The glamour and the allure were dream time for men and women alike; you didn't go to the movies to be reassured that other people had dishpan hands and varicose veins, too.

The surprising thing is that it took so long for women to figure out and resent the fact that being pampered was still being passive and patronized. The assertive women, usually played by Barbara Stanwyck or Rosalind Russell, were grossly outnumbered by the lovely ladies who stood by patiently waiting to be won. Often the career woman, brisk and successful, was herself glad to be rescued at last from the loneliness of command, grateful to have met her match and the master of her

A free spirit herself, Vanessa Redgrave played a pioneer liberated woman, dancer Isadora Duncan, in Karel Reisz' Isadora.

choice. The unique and delicate balance between her independence and their togetherness was what gave fire and charm to the teamings of Katharine Hepburn and Spencer Tracy, and that chemistry was so special that Hollywood has never found it elsewhere, then or now.

When the women were really active rather than reactive in earlier days, what we might get was Barbara Stanwyck dyed blonde and conning some weak-willed male into helping her murder her husband for the insurance money, or Gene Tierney knocking off prac-

The independent woman of many movies, husky-voiced Jean Arthur listens skeptically to Gary Cooper in Mr. Deeds Goes to Town.

tically everybody out of pure rottenness in *Leave Her to Heaven* in 1945. The villainnesses, like the villains, were apt to have all the good lines.

You remember the exceptions—the killers, the alcoholics, the brave sufferers, the steel-willed, the demented, and the raging—because if they were writ larger than life, they were also more vital and lifelike than the idea-

122

The career woman, often in tailored suits, the late Rosalind Russell played a reporter opposite Cary Grant in Howard Hawks' His Girl Friday, *which was a remake of* The Front Page *recast to allow for the element of romance.*

lized, romanticized, plasticized screen queens whose dimensions might be dreamy but did not include depth.

The compounding problem in portraying women, as in portraying men, was that the inhibitions forced on the movies by censorship gave human relationships a certain unreality, leaving them tentative and incomplete. Indeed, the objects of one's affections were likely to be as sterile as one's affections.

The new paradox is that the movies have lost their inhibitions but the women have gained very little by it in terms of roles, and have in fact lost much of their dignity. With dismayingly few exceptions the women shown in movies remain as reactive as ever, pawns and sightseers in a man's world, and the only difference is that as pawns they get shoved around a lot more brusquely than they did in the past.

The movies can now demonstrate conclusively what hell a woman's life can be. In some ways it's a useful step forward: at least a woman can be portrayed as a real person and not as an ethereal, impossible dream. But this portrait remains only a semireality, presenting us with woman's trials but still denying her the possibility of triumph and ignoring most of what she is really into and about. What the movies have yet to deal with is the flood-tide of new expectations among women who are freshly and fully conscious of their strengths and their rights, women prepared to prove and to demand their equality, women rebelling openly (or quietly and effectively) against the kind of passive, reactive, secondary roles society, and the movies, have customarily assigned them. If *My Fair Lady* is ever remade, there would probably be a terrific quarrel, either before the camera or behind it, between the hero and the heroine over who would get the right to sing "Why can't a woman be more like a man?" Certainly Eliza Doolittle has had it up to here, and Henry Higgins doesn't know the half of it.

The movies are beginning to give us hints that the ladies are not as happy as they might be, and yet there is still a time lag—two years, three years, five years, even—between the real attitudes and problems of women in our society and what is presented on the screen.

The reason, I have no doubt, is fundamentally that the movies continue to be preponderantly a male enterprise. Movies are imagined, written, financed, directed, distributed, and exhibited largely although not entirely by men, with the result that they tend to concentrate on men acting and women reacting (if indeed women are present at all). In other words, the movies continue to be about men. Because there have been so few movies about women, there is as yet no evidence that they would sell as well as or better than male-

One of the few female superstars, Audrey Hepburn got My Fair Lady *over Julie Andrews, who became a superstar anyway.*

oriented films. The runaway success of *The Sting* (virtually woman-free except for a peppering of prostitutes) reinforces the Hollywood dedication to masculine palship.

The movies *can* deal with real women, and it's interesting to look at some that have, and the results.

Alan Pakula's *Klute* (1971) won Jane Fonda a well-earned Oscar for her subtle and sensitive portrayal of a prostitute. Klute, as it happened, wasn't *her* name; she was Bree. Klute was the name of the character played by Donald Sutherland, Fonda's co-star, a dramatically important but nevertheless secondary role. (Maybe Klute looked better on marquees.) In a happy ending that would have pleased the Breen Office—like many of theirs it requires suspending disbelief—Bree abandoned her high-paying life of sin as a Manhattan call girl and went off to live as a policeman's wife in a small Pennsylvania coal-mining town. *Klute* was written by two men, and their resolution seemed not so much a resolution as a retreat to the old truth that love conquers all. Bree's willing embrace of dependence was made credible in story terms but I'm not sure the future of Bree and Klute together bears much thinking about.

Another 1971 movie, *T. R. Baskin,* gave us Candice Bergen as a beautiful and intelligent girl who liberates herself from a small town in the Midwest and goes to Chicago, only to find that Chicago isn't ready for her. She is cheated, seduced, deceived, and consigned to menial and mindless work—all by men. Concluding she is regarded only as a sex object, she decides by the end of the film to make a career of sex even though in her ten-foot scarf and Wellesley knee socks she still looks more like the Sweetheart of Sigma Chi than Shanghai Lil. Despite the supporting presences of James Caan and Peter Boyle, *T. R. Baskin* was a fairly dreadful movie. While the

Drowning in the steno pool, Candice Bergen in T. R. Baskin *felt all the frustrations women do encounter working in a male-run world.*

126

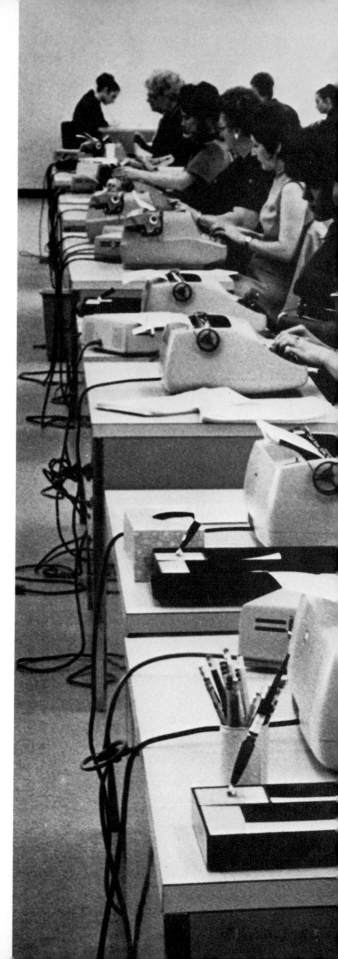

script, written by a man, acknowledges many of the sources of women's dissatisfaction, it places them in a world as superficial and diagrammatic as a crossword puzzle, burying the movie's lack of a convincing resolution behind some artful editing.

Not surprisingly, one of the most convincing expositions of the unhappiness of modern woman with her traditional role was written by one woman, Eleanor Perry, from a novel by another, Sue Kaufman. *The Diary of a Mad Housewife* (1970) erred on the far side of overstatement. Husband and wife were both exaggerations, the wife a paragon, the husband a parody. But the wife, sipping vodka to see herself through another day of thankless perfection, and the husband, a petulant, posturing fool, both bespoke the rage the writers felt about wife as drudge and husband as tyrant. (The female critics tended to find *Diary* true and trenchant; the men found it overdone. Hmm.) The paragon wife, declaring her independence, took a paramour. But she was if anything worse than before, and the message seemed to be that the madness lay in thinking she could change her luck.

Richard Brooks's *The Happy Ending* (1969) starred his wife, Jean Simmons, as a Denver housewife whose husband, a successful up-from-nothing tax accountant, is loyal, hardworking, cheerful, thrifty, brave, ambitious, clean, and obtuse. He does not see until too late that being wife-mother-hostess no longer quite satisfies his wife. She has taken to the bottle as the measure of her discontent (a subtheme that unfortunately distracted from the major impact of the film). In the end the wife has put aside both the bottle and husband John Forsythe, and the irony of the title is that there is no happy Hollywood reunion. The wife is striding off to night school and the strong inference is that she isn't coming back, certainly not until she has once again earned an identity of her own.

I suppose the ultimate liberated Hollywood woman to date has been *Myra Breckinridge* (1970), who could wear both the pants and the skirt in the family, and who discovered it is blessed both to give and to receive. But if you could take *Myra* seriously, which you couldn't, she was not a liberated figure but a creature without identity seeking not equality but revenge.

The movies have not yet shown us much of the liberated woman. In the beginning, as in such trendy works as *Getting Straight, Strawberry Statement* (both 1970), and *Drive, He Said* (1971), the liberation was defined mostly as sexual freedom. While sexual liberation is part of complete liberation, it is only part of it. As depicted in the movies, sexual liberation looked suspiciously like the old, very male dream of sex without commitment or consequence and suspiciously unlike a woman's dream of mobility and genuine equality.

But if the movies have seldom given us woman in the throes of liberation, they have often consciously or unconsciously filed depositions, as it were, that substantiate the case for liberation.

An odd, uneven movie called *Who Is Harry Kellerman and Why Is He Saying Those Terrible Things About Me?* (1971) starred Dustin Hoffman as a rags-to-riches pop songwriter whose anxieties have driven him deep into schizophrenia. His life history is strewn with the wreckage not only of his love affairs but also of his marriage (terminated because his children were a constant and intolerable reminder that he was growing older every day). His life is a sermon on the expendability of women. Although the movie is presumably intended to empathize with him, I would expect the ladies as well as the gentlemen of the jury to demand his head on a platter.

An important document (as well as a severe test of the rating system and of legal defini-

A span of sex symbols, Mae West and Raquel Welch joined in Myra Breckenridge, *a very campy ode to sexual multiplicity.*

tions of obscenity) was *Carnal Knowledge* (1971), a brutal encounter in the wars between men and women. Few movies either before or since have shown so coldly and clinically the male view of women as pure sex objects. The sense of the film, directed by Mike Nichols from a script by Jules Feiffer, was that it was impossible (and perhaps even undesirable) to have a well-rounded and meaningful relationship with a woman. It's all either bed or bored.

This film is an indictment of a certain generation and class of men and women (Ameri-

Shown here uncommonly cheerful, Jack Nicholson and Ann-Margaret were usually terribly depressed in Carnal Knowledge, *a tale of marital wars.*

can). The women are ruthless, two-timing, and emasculating or, if none of the above, plain stupid. The men are perennial captives of what Lucius Beebe once called the Italian Wet Nurse Syndrome, which still keeps *Playboy* and all its imitators solvent.

As the movie ends, the Jack Nicholson character is reduced to ever-more-impersonal and kinky sexual encounters, as if to accommodate

130

both need and revulsion simultaneously. The character Art Garfunkel plays seems to be trying for a love relationship, this time with an underage flower child. But whether he has really learned something or is simply confusing love with sex minus guilt is far from clear. Both Feiffer and Nichols seem so profoundly cynical that there is very little room for hope.

What was troubling about *Carnal Knowledge* was that, while its male case histories were all too believable, they did not seem to sustain an indictment of an entire generation, although many viewers obviously felt that they did. The unforgettable portrait from the movie is Ann-Margret as the woman desperately unhappy with a life spent as a sex object and pathetically hoping to be seen as a whole person.

Ken Russell's first successful feature, an adaptation of *Women in Love* (1969), was drawn with great fidelity from the D. H. Lawrence novel written a half-century earlier. It came close to stating an honest case for the choice, or lack of choice, that has confronted the modern woman: between marriage, on the one hand, and a sense of personal identity—with the rights of individual assertion and achievement—on the other. Oliver Reed and Alan Bates made the running, but Glenda Jackson is the relevant, troubling figure.

John Schlesinger's *Sunday Bloody Sunday* (1972) was not really about the woman character (again played by Glenda Jackson): the protagonist, caught in the tearing apex of a triangle, was Peter Finch. Jackson was, however, moving in her portrayal of a woman who already knows that the satisfactions of career are not in themselves enough, but who also knows painfully well that a bad marriage is *not* better than none. And if she did not, as we watched, resolve her dilemma, it was at least set forth: how to balance the security of love and marriage with mobility and career.

She had not won, but she had not been defeated, either; and if there was accordingly a note of hope at the end, it was simply that she knew, as the Peter Finch character knew, that you go on, that life goes on.

The same thin but resolute hope colored the ending of *Rachel, Rachel* (1968), whose title role was played by Joanne Woodward. It examined the life of an unmarried small-town schoolteacher who was not yet resigned to spinsterhood but beginning to be an eccentric. Stewart Stern's careful script and Paul Newman's direction revealed the particular personality and the universally recognizable type, the woman too intelligent to conceal anything from herself about the frustrating, deadening sameness of the life that lay ahead of her unless she made a move, almost any move.

In *The Prime of Miss Jean Brodie* (1969), from a sharp novella by Muriel Spark that was later adapted for the stage, Maggie Smith presented another kind of spinster schoolteacher, in her own loneliness and frustration retreating dangerously into dreams of power and leadership through which she and her adoring pupils will somehow uphold ancient ideals in a different world. At that, Jean Brodie was notable because she was self-willed, even if she seemed destined for collapse and madness at the end of her chosen path. Far more often the women in contemporary films are seen as victims, usually of circumstances over which society gives them no control.

Karen Black as the Monkey in Ernest Lehman's unsuccessful adaptation of the Philip Roth novel *Portnoy's Complaint* (1972) was the most persuasive, which is to say the least caricatured, character in the film—open, direct, and spontaneous, a part of Portnoy's life because she is sexually free yet doomed to be only a bed partner because he cannot deal with her honesty. She will survive (better than he will, it seems clear) but it is not cer-

Celebrating life (overleaf) *Glenda Jackson in* Women in Love *defied the rules of society.*

Ellen Burstyn as a woman obsessed with problems of her fading youth still managed a show of spirit in The King of Marvin Gardens.

tain that she will find a man who will appreciate her as the complete human being she knows herself to be. As the street-wise woman she is, she may be able to turn chauvinism to her advantage and support, but it is not the resolution she would prefer.

Ellen Burstyn as Bruce Dern's mistress in *The King of Marvin Gardens* (1972), a cool, original, stylish, and little-seen film by Robert Rafelson, was a slightly senior version of the Monkey, consigned to kept-woman status, making extravagant demands and striking bombastic attitudes to assert her worth. The terrors of middle age, which seem to herald her failure as a woman and even to threaten her status as a courtesan (a word almost wildly inappropriate to her life in a gloomy out-of-season Atlantic City hotel), drive her to burn her cosmetics and clothes in a bizarre scene on the beach, a symbolic suicide.

Peter Bogdanovich's first major homage to the movies, *The Last Picture Show* (1971), was peopled with cinemythic figures, characters drawn not so much from life as from the movies Bogdanovich admired, so that they were visions of a vision of life. Cloris Leachman, the dowdy, ignored, love-starved wife of the high-school coach, is a prototypical figure in American life. Making a last, dying clutch at romance with a high school boy, she had a wan, beseeching intensity more haunting than anything else about the film. The glimpse of a thin life, wasteful and wasted seen against what she might have been and done, proves unforgettable, a performance and a slice of life that transcended the film conventions Bogdanovich was celebrating.

George Lucas' *American Graffiti* (1973) was essentially an autobiographical excursion, impressionistic, funny, and affecting, into his and his pals' past. The girls existed in the boys' lives; it was, as always, not the other way around. But the girls (except for the mysterious and probably allegorical blonde in the classic T-bird) were exactly drawn. The Cindy Williams character, the prom queen clinging so tightly to her steady that she is distraught when he wants room to breathe, is a curious prediction of the Cloris Leachman role in *The Last Picture Show*, racing for the happy-ever-

A brief, wistful romance with Timothy Bottoms was probably a last chance for ailing Cloris Leachman in The Last Picture Show.

after marriage and likely as not to find it the end of promise rather than the beginning.

Ingmar Bergman's masterful *Cries and Whispers,* released in America in 1973, was almost an anthology of women's states; and although it was set in a vague turn-of-the-century period, one sensed that Bergman's intention was to remove the story from specific time rather than establish it in time. His somber, brooding study of two sisters come to witness the last hours of a third mixed the realities of present and past, and his theme was love—given, denied, absent, remembered, lost. The film's most corrosive portrait was of Ingrid Thulin as a woman trapped in a loveless and hateful marriage who is moved (in her fantasy? Bergman is ambiguous) to mutilate herself with a broken wine glass. Liv Ullmann is a sensualist, spoiled and self-indulgent, driving her husband to attempt suicide (apparently). Yet she seems not really willful or amoral but, in her own terms, as isolated and stifled as her sister by the decorative and empty roles society assigns them. The dying sister (Harriett Andersson) has survived on faith and the love she has been able give, and if she is saintly she is also a martyr. But she has sustained her faith and known love, and Bergman counts her blessings.

(Bergman has said that *Cries and Whispers* began with his wish to do a portrait of his mother, and that each of the women—the three sisters and the dying sister's maid, played by Kari Sylwan—are aspects of his mother's life and personality. Each of the four characterizations is fully developed and rings with emotional truth.)

Cinderella Liberty (1973), filmed by Mark Rydell from the novel and screenplay by Darryl Ponicsan, was not entirely convincing. Its ending in particular was unbelievably tidy and optimistic after all that had gone before. Yet Marsha Mason gave a believable portrayal, as pungent as cheap perfume, of one of the sorriest losers the movies have recently shown us. She was a second-generation dockside saloon girl, pool-sharking, hustling drinks, and entertaining short-time visitors in her sleazy hotel suite—all to sustain herself and her illegitimate half-black son. In the end she deserts her son, an act of nobility, it seems, because she is leaving him in the better care of James Caan, a nice, medium-bright sailor who loves them both. There is a strong implication that all three of them will soon be together again, beginning all over in New Orleans. But Mason has been too convincing as the smote-down Cinderella, the born loser who has been given a tantalizing look at better times but who can't quite grasp them. Her departure can also be seen as a last act of irresponsibility, perhaps born of despair but still a foolish flight toward the freedom that is bound to lie at the end of the bus ticket. And actually the portrait of a wrecked woman is stronger, scarier, and probably more accurate if it remains consistent, without the arbitrary and dubious effort to build in an upbeat ending.

The same kind of attempt to paste a happy ending over the unhappy realities previously established also blurred the image of *Alice Doesn't Live Here Any More* (1974), which Martin Scorsese directed from an original script by Robert Getchell. For much of its length it was an electrically dramatized but fundamentally well-observed account of a woman unexpectedly freed from the bonds of a lousy marriage and enabled to discover that the alternatives are as bad or worse. Ellen Burstyn, who won the Oscar as best actress for the performance, has dreamed of being a big-band vocalist. She has settled for marriage —any marriage—because that's the accepted role and the only security for the woman who hasn't made it as a big-band singer, or even as a cocktail-bar pianist. The marriage—to a sullen slob of a soft-drink delivery man—is a bad charade, solved by his accidental death.

The woman as loser, Marsha Mason was a hard-luck bar girl and pool hustler finding a measure of love with James Caan in Cinderella Liberty.

Now, with her foul-mouthed but endearing twelvish son, she sets forth from dreary New Mexico toward old dreams revisited. She gets a job playing piano in a saloon that would seem hardly able to sustain a juke box, and is seduced by a sadistic creep who also turns out to be married. She flees again to a job as a waitress in a high-velocity hash house. Her control over her life (and her son) is slipping through her rough, red hands and it looks bad until a rich, sensible, marriageable, and smitten rancher (warmly played by Kris Kristofferson) ambles in for eggs over easy. There are vicissitudes and false stops, but finally there is a shouted profession of love amidst the rush-hour clatter of crockery and hysterical short-order cooks in the beanery. (It is a scene Howard Hawks might have got away with in 1938, if the whole film had been moving along the same antic lines.) Once again, marriage looks better than anything. But even though this marriage looks better than the other, it is still a marriage of refuge, a consolation for dreams not realized, goals not achieved, a personal assertion not made.

There was sharp detailing along the way, and Getchell's script particularly caught the camaraderie that often arises among women in the face of their common adversary, men. The friendship between Burstyn and Diane Ladd, as a salty and supportive waitress, was a notable ingredient in the film. There is the gray look of reality in the pictures of the constant but constantly bored wife and the far-from-merry widow (trained to do little, hard put to find even mindless work, vulnerable to almost any attentive male). The ending, in which marriage is presented as an either/or alternative to a career, is almost a grotesquely Hollywood happy ending. If there are meant to be overtones of irony, a weak surrender to the status quo, the tones are beyond the range of hearing. But up until then, for all its larger-than-life inventions, *Alice* conveyed a number

Waiting for someone to love, friends Diane Ladd and Ellen Burstyn shared their gripes and dreams in Alice Doesn't Live Here Anymore.

Trying for perfection as a housewife and mother, the Gena Rowlands character in John Cassavetes' Woman Under the Influence *drove herself into a nervous breakdown.*

of home truths about woman's lot in lower Middle America.

And so, even more balefully, did John Cassavetes in *A Woman Under the Influence* (1974), in which his own wife, Gena Rowlands, gave a high-intensity and disturbing characterization as a Los Angeles housewife spinning into a nervous breakdown. What the root causes of the breakdown are is not made explicit; the viewer is in a sense invited to pick them out in the fabric of the life style.

What seems to be true is that the wife is caught between the pressures of marriage as it is and marriage as she imagines it ought to be. Nervous, imaginative, fanciful, she pursues some impossible vision of perfection, as airy and impractical as her husband's grasp on life is flat-footed and practical. He is a construction-gang boss, loyal, loving, but too thick-witted to know how to deal with his hummingbird of a wife. There is a barracuda-like mother-in-law, too malevolent to be true, and a hapless family doctor whose competence does not include an ability to deal with a woman at the end of her frazzled ropes.

Much of the movie is as hard to endure as fingernails raking across a blackboard. It is partly (although only partly) because Rowlands makes the suffering of the wife so palpable and affecting. It is partly because Cassavetes's technique can impose pain of a different kind. Scenes that are not actually improvised feel like improvisation because they strain story logic and force the actors to work unimaginably hard to wrench them into life. Overextended scenes and the use of actors simply unable to handle the emotional demands of the scenes make *A Woman Under the Influence* painful as craft as well as story. Yet the result ultimately is to make the Rowlands character even more powerfully touching and tragic. The intensity is so acute that her collapse leaves us unsure whether or not the gap between life and art has closed.

And although Cassavetes, too, provides a guardedly happy ending—the woman returned, shaky but clear-eyed, to the bosom of her family—the happiness seems tentative and tenuous. It is impossible to see or to say what has changed fundamentally. She has returned to a husband who loves her without having the faintest idea where her head is and who is incapable of giving her the kind of reassurance and encouragement she is going to need. Love does not necessarily conquer all, a new

The black family experience in the comedy
Claudine *had Diahann Carroll and her brood*
bravely starting anew with James Earl Jones.

message from the screen that Cassavetes may
or may not have intended. In any event, the
Rowlands-Cassavetes portrait of a modern
woman has seldom been equaled for depth
and compassion. She is wholly unique, and
yet she is part of any number of women each
of us has known.

The problems of the black woman in
American society are particular, and have rarely been dealt with at any level. *Claudine*
(1974) was startling and commendable not
simply because it explored the life of a black
woman, but because the results were at once
funny and incisive. Lester and Tina Pine in
their script fashioned a romantic comedy of
bitter materials. Diahann Carroll made an uncommonly elegant maid (concealing her jobs
from the welfare bureaucrats) but she brought
it off, and so did James Earl Jones as the dashing trash collector who becomes the man in
her life. The surfaces were romantic but sheer,
and beneath them were the realities of a ghet-
toized society within the broader society,
made matriarchal by a welfare system that
emasculates the men and makes deception a
way of life. The system is a symptom of the
inequalities and prejudices of society as a
whole, but *Claudine* left no doubt that the

Invoking the mood of intense personal despair, Ingmar Bergman instructs Liv Ullmann, who plays a psychiatrist on the verge of emotional collapse in Face to Face.

system was also generating its own miseries, reinforcing a dependent life style by penalizing ambition. Once again, a buoyant happy ending, even if you wanted most fervently to believe it, seemed contradicted by everything that had gone before. But the defiant and assertive charm of Claudine, her family, and her man was tonic and positive, and the miracle of the movie was that bitter truths could be made so palatable.

Despite the occasional star turn, such as Barbra Streisand in *Funny Lady* (1975) or *A Star Is Born* (1976), the screen's women have continued to be victims not victors, and in both of the Streisand outings, her triumphs were clouded by the loneliness of stardom.

More often, although sympathetically seen, the woman, any woman, is also a sufferer. In Ingmar Bergman's *Face to Face* (1976), Liv Ullmann gave a nerve-shredding performance as a psychiatrist plunging into a nervous breakdown and a failed suicide attempt. The destructive forces in her life include a dull and loveless marriage, meaningless and unsupportive love affairs, a despairing sense of her own powerlessness as a healer. Her collapse is triggered by a visit to the home of her grandparents with all its heavy associations with childhood, and her nightmare hallucinations move her back into childhood. (The screams are primal; Bergman is fascinated by the primal scream therapy of Dr. Arthur Janov.)

In the end, Ullmann has recovered (not only from the breakdown but also from the shock of being raped) and is confidently returning to work. But as in some of the other films about women, the happy ending is much less persuasive than the accounting of the troubles. It is so quick and pat in *Face to Face* that a viewer could be forgiven for suspecting that Bergman had written it that way to provide reassurance for himself as well as for his audience.

Faye Dunaway in *Chinatown* (1975), written by Robert Towne and directed by Roman Polanski, was a mystery woman whose tragic secret was that she had an incestuous child by her own father. By the time of *Network*, late in 1976, Dunaway was in charge of her own destiny, but as a ruthlessly ambitious television executive incapable of love and deterred by nothing on her push to success (measured in ratings). She was a cartoon of the career woman and, even in success, a victim, this time of her own self-destructive drives. You may not lose, but you can't win.

Once in the rarest of whiles there has been a heroine like Carol Kane in Joan Micklin Silver's period piece *Hester Street* (1975), about Jewish immigrant life in Manhattan in the 1890s. The heroine, arriving to join a husband she finds no longer loves her, not only gets out of the marriage on her own terms but lands the right new man and uses her divorce settlement to launch them on a new and prosperous life in the new world. Mrs. Silver's small, low-budget, black and white film has enjoyed a large success, but the possibility (strong) that its positive and triumphant heroine was a factor in the success seems not yet to have struck Hollywood.

A woman's film, adapted and directed by Joan Micklin Silver, Hester Street *featured Carol Kane as an immigrant wife arriving to start a new life in the 1890s in New York.*

The opening up of the screen has made it possible to get closer to the truths of all our lives, but perhaps of women's most particularly. If until now the movies have made only tentative use of the possibilities and told only a part of the whole truth, we are at least at a beginning. The movies have been in a revolutionary condition but so have the lives and thoughts of women, and sooner than later the two revolutions are going to intersect.

Heroes, anti-heroes, and pals, pals, pals

The movies were made for action, which is also to say that they were made for heroics. From the beginning the principal pursuit of the movies was to create characters on the grand scale—larger-than-life heroes, rascals, and villains, and every now and then, heroines.

Heroes. From William S. Hart through a rangeful of cowboys to John Wayne. Doug Fairbanks to Gable and Tracy and Cooper, Bogart and Peck and Newman and Redford and Eastwood. Yet even as the list is brought into present time, a marked difference becomes evident. Up to the time of Spencer Tracy, heroic actors as villains were unthinkable. James Cagney was an exception, although even his villains were supersized and strangely sympathetic. Another was Humphrey Bogart, who could be a villain, and a hateful one, as in *The Petrified Forest* (1936), which made his fame, and *The Roaring Twenties* (1939).

The later heroes grow shaded; they are heroes often but not always. Steve McQueen has said he will not play villains, although he has played rascals, victims, and heroic losers. Robert Redford along with his good guys has played weak men (as in *The Way We Were* in 1973) and nonheroic winners, in *Downhill Racer* (1969) and *The Candidate* (1972), which left one uneasily unsure what kind of man the winner would turn out to be once he took office.

Paul Newman, although closer to the public's image of the traditional screen superhero than any other contemporary actor, has also played villains, and crackingly well, as in *Hud* in 1963. In *Cool Hand Luke* (1967), Newman extended the tradition of antihero, the existential hero, that Bogart had pioneered almost single-handedly. Newman's Luke is an amiable drifter, a live-and-let-live gent who runs afoul of the law by attacking parking meters because they represent authority and place limits on individual freedom. He ends up on a chain gang (the movie indicated that all too little had changed since Mervyn Leroy

The principal romantic hero of his generation, Paul Newman (sitting pretty in Butch Cassidy) *has also played many complex and unsympathetic characters as in* Hud.

144

made *I Am a Fugitive from a Chain Gang* thirty-five years earlier). He dies for his belief in the right to be let alone, a reluctant hero who lost—or perhaps broke even, as his principal tormentor dies too.

What the movies did to men in the post-television years was not really different in spirit from the depedestalizing of women, the move that Molly Haskell capsulized in the title of her book *From Reverence to Rape.*

Surely the most glamorous of all blue-collar heroes, Steve McQueen, here a speeding Bullitt, *has excelled as a man who gets things done.*

The hero suddenly turned out to have feet of clay. The element that remained the same, however, was that men were still the central figures more often than not. And that they were portrayed, despite any flaws and failings, with a sympathetic understanding and depth

The character actor as a superstar, Dustin Hoffman, here a songwriter in Harry Kellerman, *ranges from graduates to grifters.*

of insight not afforded women. The central figure was just that, the central figure, but he was not necessarily a hero; he could be an antihero, a nonhero, or a case history. For a while it was not only the English film *Morgan* (1966) that could be subtitled "A Suitable Case for Treatment." There were a lot of treatable cases around, including Dustin Hoffman as the songwriter dissolving into schizophrenia in *Who Is Harry Kellerman and Why Is He*

Saying Those Terrible Things About Me? (1971) and Sean Connery, who in *A Fine Madness* (1966) is treated to a prefrontal lobotomy but emerges the same mad poet as before. Jack Nicholson and Art Garfunkel were both clinical studies in *Carnal Knowledge*, and Ni-

147

cholson, a year later, in *The King of Marvin Gardens* (1972), portrayed a different kind of man but one who is also operating close to the boundary of sanity.

The men who once were heroes get into terrible and often demeaning troubles. Yet there is no question that they have come off far better in the movies than women have. They are somehow seen in the whole circumstance of their lives. The character Jack Lemmon played in *Save the Tiger* (1973) is not a sympathetic figure; he has become a procurer for his business clients and turned crook to save the firm. Even so, he is viewed sympathetically, and we share his bafflement over how a nice hardworking guy could have drifted out so far. Finally we see his loss of innocence not as a private dilemma but as a national tragedy, the snuffing out of that special, buoyant, optimistic American spirit.

An American Everyman, Jack Lemmon moved from light comedy to dramatic roles, like his tired corrupted businessman in Save the Tiger.

The movies are full of sharply delineated portraits of modern men under duress. The ever-present Jack Nicholson captured the anxieties of a generation in *Five Easy Pieces* (1970). His protagonist was an oil-field roughneck pretending to be nothing more than an easygoing laborer, although he has really dropped out from an affluent and culturally prominent family, rejecting what was evidently a promising career as a pianist. So far as we can tell, it is more comfortable for him to have tried, to have beaten failure to the punch by accepting it without ever risking success. There was an aimlessness in his life, a paralysis induced partly by his fear of trying and partly by his feeling that there were no goals worth seeking.

The man Brando portrayed in *Last Tango in Paris* (1972) was in some ways the same person in *Five Easy Pieces*. But in *Tango* he has seen more of life, lived longer, and after years of rootless wandering has found, and briefly had, a place in the sun and made a commitment. Now he has lost it all and he is near death. Whether the death is literal or symbolic does not matter; it is all the same.

These figures can be taken as particular or universal, but either way they are credible and affecting; they exist in and respond to a recognizable world. Often, indeed, the men are caught in changing times and have come to realize that society has begun operating under new ground rules, ones that they don't yet fully understand. The character George Segal plays in *Blume in Love* (1973) understands the permissive society well enough to enjoy its trimmings, but he is unhappy in it and eager for some older constancies. Harvey Keitel as the hero of the Martin Scorsese film *Mean Streets* (1973) knows that the rest of the world is changing, but he appears to have no choice except to stay within the Italian-American enclave in New York, with its elder-dominated caste system and its codes of behavior, now inappropriate and outdated.

The movies have proven that they can look at modern man's life in the full range of its traumas and triumphs. But they don't necessarily want to, and seem to be wanting to less and less. The trend toward palship and tan-

Pals in a fast-changing West, Paul Newman and Robert Redford, Butch Cassidy and The Sundance Kid *confirmed their star status and made the partnership a Hollywood staple.*

dem heroes, launched in 1969 by *Butch Cassidy and the Sundance Kid*, looks nearly a decade later to be as durable as crabgrass.

Palship is not new in the movies. Comedy was often a team effort, and there were all the swell-guy pals, epitomized by Spencer Tracy and Clark Gable, either fighting each other or fighting for each other, enjoying a robust and innocent togetherness except

when they were eyeing the same lady. There were other palships, including Pat O'Brien's and James Cagney's, that only the electric chair could—and did—end.

The succession of films with pals as protagonists now is long enough to be astounding, and puzzling. It is not limited to romantic melodrama such as *Butch Cassidy* or to romantic comedy like *The Sting* (1973), which was designed as a commercial rehash of *Butch Cassidy* minus any meaningful content. (Romantic is probably the wrong word at that, as Katharine Ross was more a shared convenience than a true love of either of the boys, while in *The Sting* there was no love interest at all, only a succession of hookers, one of them murderous.)

Midnight Cowboy (1969) had its nonheroic twin heroes, and what was interesting about this film was that, despite the cowboy's determination to be a stud hustler, there was no overt suggestion that he and Ratso were anything but friends in need. Even in a sexually sensitized movie era, the male comradeships continue to be as asexual as they were in the uptight thirties. The only latent desires seem to be those of the producers to find audiences. The boys, lest anyone get the wrong ideas, are indeed aggressively heterosexual, as in *Scarecrow* (1973), in which Al Pacino and Gene Hackman make their sporting way cross country toward their ultimate goals of a car wash and a lost wife. The women are used, and Pacino's wife turns out to have been abused. But Hackman and Pacino break through their defenses and find they care about each other; perhaps the consolation for the women is that if men are capable of caring for each other they may, someday, be capable of caring for women.

The three sailors of *The Last Detail*, the two pals of *Mean Streets*, the two chance-met young men of *Bad Company*, George Segal and Elliott Gould as the compulsive gamblers

Naval escorts for soon-to-be prisoner Randy Quaid in The Last Detail *were Otis Young and versatile Jack Nicholson, a superstar after long service in low-budget action pictures.*

of Robert Altman's *California Split,* the loyal
pitcher and the dying catcher of *Bang the
Drum Slowly,* the inmates of *The Longest
Yard,* and the young rustlers (Jeff Bridges and
Sam Waterson) of *Rancho Deluxe*—all films
from the early seventies—appear to live in societies in which substantive relationships with
women are impossible or undesirable or both.

The Great Waldo Pepper (1975), a second
attempt to catch the *Butch Cassidy/Sting*
magic, although this time with Redford flying
solo in World War I airplanes, once again
is about a man's world. The women in the
film are ornamental and expendable.

The unkindest dig of all is that women are
not only regarded as extraneous in the palship
picture, they are sometimes depicted as nothing but trouble. Sean Connery and Michael
Caine would probably still be ruling that
mythical mountain kingdom northwest of
India, in the John Huston telling of Rudyard
Kipling's *The Man Who Would Be King*
(1975), if Connery hadn't chased after the
wrong lady. (It remains one of the best and
most colorful of the pal epics, a proper homage to its classic source.)

The Missouri Breaks (1976) was not a palship picture: Jack Nicholson and Marlon
Brando as its co-stars were deadly enemies
whose final stalking combat could be said to
have been instigated, obliquely anyway, by
Kathleen Lloyd as the woman in both their
lives, one way or another. The movie failed
critically and commercially, probably because
there seemed to have been so little reason for
making it except to make money. It is possible
that, by a nice irony, the movie would have
worked better if the two stars had been bud-
dies not opponents. Then again there is nothing to be gained by encouraging a formula
that has lost its freshness and, more to the
point, has made it difficult to find support
for other and less hackneyed story devices.

*A fast-rising star, Al Pacino gained his first big
acclaim as Marlon Brando's favorite son and heir
in* The Godfather *and its sequel.*

152

At that the palship ploy survives even leaden flops like *Harry and Walter Go to New York* (1976) with James Caan and Elliot Gould as vaudevillian con men, as it also survives admirable but unprofitable works like *Scarecrow*, whose melodramatic finale (Pacino going berserk in a freezing public fountain) was evidently too grim for the audience.

It is clear from the grumblings any critic hears that not all women are pleased by the prevalence of man-centered movies or the scarcity of movies that deal intelligently and sympathetically with women. Yet the movie audience, whatever else one may say about it, is roughly balanced between the sexes; and while a few of the pal films have failed, enough have succeeded to keep the form alive.

Surveys suggest that women make the majority of the decisions about what movies they (and their fathers, sons, husbands, brothers, or lovers) will see. So one explanation for the ongoing male dominance of the screen is that women are glad enough to watch the romantic superstars—Redford, Newman, Caine, and the others—even as they wish for a new generation of leading women. The other explanation is that the success of the movies about men is not preference but lack of effective choice. Those who make movies, clinging to any evidence that appears to support a decision they have already made, give the public what it has shown it wanted before. Nothing changes until the public demonstrates that it wants a change.

The buddy movies reflect, among other things, a lingering immaturity among many American males in their relationships with women. A retreat to palship in everyday life is demonstrably related to a reluctance to make commitments if not to an outright fear of and insecurity in the presence of women. But, seen in those terms, the problem is almost certainly generational, for a younger age

A pair of now historic bikers, Dennis Hopper and Peter Fonda (with Luke Askew hitching) found it hard to repeat the success of Easy Rider *—stardom is perishable.*

group seems able to handle its relationships with a good deal more directness, ease, and trust. Because the same generation is also the principal audience for the movies, one wonders why it sits so passively through demonstrations of the way things were. For the moment, however, the movies are a delayed-action mirror, and it is the movie decision makers who are reflecting their own graying images in that mirror.

Are the stars out tonight, or in?

Critics do see the movies as a progression of directors, from Griffith to Godard and beyond, by way of Eisenstein and Ford. But even the most austere of the critics would almost certainly have to admit that what made true film believers of them in the beginning were the stars: Lillian Gish dying so young in *Broken Blossoms*, Chaplin mournfully munching an old shoe in *The Gold Rush*, Harold Lloyd clinging to the hands of a clock a hair-raising distance above the street in *Safety Last*, Clark Gable showing Claudette Colbert how to hitchhike in *It Happened One Night*, Vivien Leigh clutching the rich red earth of Tara in *Gone with the Wind*, Humphrey Bogart telling Sam to play "As Time Goes By" in *Casablanca* (really, Bogart doing anything), John Wayne heroically acknowledging his own heroics in *True Grit*, Barbra Streisand warning the rain to stay away from her parade in *Funny Girl*, Robert Redford and Paul Newman conning us all in *The Sting*.

The star system began to take shape even before the movies were out of their awkward, fixed-camera infancy. Throughout the four-score years since, in silence and in speech, the stars have remained the principal source of growth, durability, and allure for the medium.

D. W. Griffith discovered, among other things, the movies' first female superstar, the delicate Canadian girl who took the name Mary Pickford. Charlie Chaplin was the first male superstar, although that term does not even begin to describe him. He was not merely an enormously popular performer: he was a creative genius who did much to define the potential of the movies by giving broad comedy the extra dimension of depth.

The incredible popularity of Pickford and Chaplin fetched them weekly salaries that were beyond the dreams of emperors and empresses. America's Sweetheart and the Tramp also set the stars in their courses as the central ingredient of the movies. They made it inevitable for the movies to grow into a major in-

"We had faces then," said Gloria Swanson in film Sunset Boulevard, *and so did youthful Gary Cooper and Marlene Dietrich in Frank Borzage's* Desire *in 1936.*

156

dustry, to be moved from homes in penny arcades and converted storefronts to splendid picture palaces.

Pickford and Chaplin were identifiable personalities who transcended their particular roles; they were looked up to because they had qualities their audiences admired or wanted to possess. In this, they defined what the movie star was and has remained ever since: a projection of the moviegoer's own dreams, an idealization of the person the viewer wants to be.

Chaplin remains in a class by himself. Chaplin's Tramp, in his dusty derby, baggy pants, undersized tailcoat, and oversized bottomless shoes, was a paradox with a cane. He was weak and foolish yet resolute and fearlessly noble. He was as timorous as an old man, yet full of brave mischief, ready to take on the town bully to protect an innocent maiden. He was a born loser who triumphed in the end or, if not triumphant, was at least never defeated, always able to walk jauntily away. He was a chivalrous dandy in need of a shoeshine, an embodiment of all the virtues of kindness and self-sacrifice that we would like to find in ourselves.

Our wishes and dreams have changed considerably over the years and so, accordingly, have the kinds of actors and actresses who are now stars. Today the attributes that make a star go beyond talent and physical appearance; they are, rather, concerned with interior qualities (real or imagined) that say a good deal not only about the stars but about their audiences, and about the times in which we all live.

Even in these days of movie revivals, it is not easy to have access to a wide variety of silent films. It therefore is no accident that the starry names that come quickest to mind are Rudolph Valentino, Clara Bow, Theda Bara, John Gilbert, Alla Nazimova, Douglas Fairbanks, Sr., and the noblest profile of them all, Francis X. Bushman. There were dozens

of others. What links all of them is that they seemed both off-screen and on to be creatures of make-believe—extravagant, exotic, larger than life, guaranteed to transport us away from the humdrum at the speed of arc light, at eighteen frames per second. There was the suggestion of lives lived to the throbbing tempo of the tango, of tempestuous romances, and of Pierce-Arrows driven at devil-may-care speeds.

Whether legend and reality matched didn't much matter, but more often than not they probably did. Fame had a way of making the stars the captives as well as the creators of their legends.

There exists a touching testimony on the star as captive in a report by Henry L. Mencken on a dinner he once had with Rudolph Valentino, at Valentino's invitation. A Chicago newspaper had complained editorially that Valentino's image as a suave and highly fragranced lover was unforgivably popular and bound to turn all American men into effeminate dandies. Valentino, depressed and furious, had turned to Mencken for guidance. Mencken, alas, could only advise Valentino to tell them all to go to hell.

"A curiously naive and boyish young fellow," Mencken wrote later, after Valentino's death at the age of thirty one, "with a disarming air of inexperience. . . . Valentino's agony was the agony of a man of relatively civilized feelings thrown into a situation of intolerable vulgarity, destructive alike to his peace and to his dignity. It was not that trifling Chicago episode that was riding him; it was the whole grotesque futility of his life. . . . Here was a young man who was living daily the dream of millions of other young men. Here was one who was catnip to women. Here was one who had wealth and fame. And here was one who was very unhappy."

Not all the stars were so unhappy, although many found it hard to cope with the kind of money, attention, and adulation that few

The immortal Chaplin, a Cockney-born music hall comedian, made his tramp a universally loved symbol of the little guy with a pure heart and a gift for mischief.

158

men and women in the history of the world had ever known. The suicides, the crack-ups, and the drop-outs were also part of the legendry of early film stars. But they did much to make the twenties seem to roar, and Valentino managed to hide his unhappiness from the camera, and from his fans. He and his generation of stars were catnip to a relatively unsophisticated mass audience that wanted its leading men and ladies to live extravagant, naughty, daring lives so that it could vicariously indulge in the wicked good life too.

The immortal screen-lover, Rudolph Valentino, wooing Agnes Ayres in The Sheik *in 1926 is in vogue again a half-century after his death.*

Mencken's tone in talking about the movies ("intolerable vulgarity," "grotesque futility") reflected prevailing intellectual attitudes toward them, although I suspect that even then there was a difference between public protestation and private practice. The poet Vachel Lindsay was an early serious film critic, and a whole generation of American novelists was

to be deeply influenced by the visual experience of the movies, as any page of Ernest Hemingway, F. Scott Fitzgerald, or John O'Hara is likely to show.

There were other currents in filmmaking in the 1920s—a brief, brilliant flowering of expressionism in the German cinema, Sergei Eisenstein's achievements in montage within a Soviet cinema conceived as an implement of public policy, Jean Renoir's early triumphs of poetic realism in France. Even in Hollywood an occasional serious film was released along

Rising and falling stars, Joan Crawford and John Gilbert co-starred in Four Walls *in 1928. She was just beginning; he became one of the casualties of movies that talked.*

with the likes of *One Stolen Night* and *Lying Lips*—King Vidor's somber and powerful social dramas, *The Crowd* and *The Big Parade*, for example, whose themes outweighed the name value of the players. But Vidor's works were a silent minority. Attractive stars running through generally escapist plots earned

Star and star-maker, Anita King, "The Paramount Girl" receives instructions about a publicity tour from Cecil B. De Mille, who was her director on The Virginian *in 1914.*

Hollywood films their preeminent place in the world market.

And, inevitably, as the movies became big business, the stars were institutionalized into a system. The studios, led by MGM, signed whole rosters of contract players, from superstars to hopefuls. The group photograph of the Metro family gathered for a luncheon to celebrate the studio's twenty-fifth birthday in 1949 is still awesome proof of the number and luminosity of the stars who belonged to the House of Mayer.

Stars were money, and the object of the system as it evolved in the 1930s was to discov-er and groom new stars, transforming pneumatic high school girls and toothy gas-station attendants into tomorrow's idols. Yet the truth is it was the system itself that mattered, more than the stars it created. The system recognized the unique truth about the movies: they did not simply make dreams, they *were* the dream. They were the most spectacular escape route man had yet devised to get

A trio of stars, Cary Grant, Katharine Hepburn, and James Stewart made Philadelphia Story *a very sophisticated comedy. George Cukor directed.*

away from poverty, mean labor, small-town dullness, and big-city anonymity. Running away with the circus was a fantasy that offered freedom, mobility, and a certain rakish esteem; making it in the movies promised all that plus fame and incalculable fortune, with no animal cages to clean out.

The fan magazines spawned by the dozens in the late teens and twenties played to those fantasies, celebrating not only the stars but the possibility of stardom. And while every generality admits exceptions, it seems that the vampy, sheiky, exotic giants of the 1920s began to be undone not only by sound (which

gave away the secrets of heavy accents and squeaky voices) but by rather more domestic romantic types. These later stars were just as handsome or beautiful as their predecessors, but they were more accessible to the average moviegoer, who could believe they had used acting in films to escape from the boredom next door.

James Cagney, honored in 1974 at what may have been the most affectionate banquet

ever held in Hollywood, gave wry thanks for "that touch of the gutter" in his hard-times childhood, without which, he said, his career would not have been possible. He wasn't wrong. It was his streetside projection of a feisty guy with a heart of gold and temper of red who would have lived in the tenement around the corner that—with Cagney's meticulous and inspired command of his art—created such a strong bond with his audience. Without that bond stardom does not occur.

Although James Stewart came to Hollywood via Broadway and Princeton University out of a boyhood in the prosperous Pennsylvania middle class, from 1935 forward he was the screen's epitome of the small-town young man—awkward but idealistic, naive but not dumb, ill at ease in sophisticated society but infinitely superior to it.

The women might be (virtually always were) stunningly pretty, but in Joan Crawford, Barbara Stanwyck, Carole Lombard, Joan Blondell, Ginger Rogers, Ann Sheridan, Betty Grable, Rita Hayworth, and even, slightly later, Elizabeth Taylor, there was never a hint of foreign air or forbidding hauteur. These were the girls who had lived next door (if you were very fortunate) but had left town as soon as they could, possibly trailing a spicy rumor or two. They may have seemed inaccessible because of their glamour, but otherwise they were not different from "ordinary" girls.

Katharine Hepburn was special, and those drawling New England accents with the wall-to-wall A's said aristocrat very loudly indeed. But she was always the maverick aristocrat, disgusted with the snobberies and rituals of her own kind, always ready to scrap the proprieties in a good cause. Bette Davis was also special, as indeed she and Katharine Hepburn still are. As the most versatile actress of her screen generation, Davis could be a malevolent alley cat in *Of Human Bondage* or queen to an emperor in *Juarez* with equal authority.

Those two great continental imports, Greta Garbo and Charles Boyer co-starred in Conquest *in 1937; she left the movies four years later.*

Best of the screen actresses was Bette Davis, here in All This and Heaven, Too *in 1940.*

Marlene Dietrich: legs and exotic allure.

Of all the stars who came out of the studios in the 1930s, Clark Gable was rightly called the King, the most popular of them all because he came closest to filling a particular vision of perfection for the audience. He had risen from nothing to everything without (as far as anyone could tell) sacrificing his independence or masculinity. For an audience that did not always admire or approve of everything it heard about movie stars, part of Gable's appeal was that he seemed to view Gable the Film Star with a kind of half-amused, half-chagrined detachment, as if parading before the camera was not quite the sort of thing a grown man ought to be doing. Our impression of his bemusement made his roles somehow seem all the more virile and credible.

Gable was the American dream with a moustache, the rough-hewn man of outdoor action, the lumberjack, wildcatter, barnstorming pilot, soldier of fortune, adventurer, and he was credible and dignified as a world-weary wrangler in his last film, *The Misfits*, completed just before he died at fifty-nine in 1960. He looked splendid in ascots and miserable in neckties, and he seemed crowded and restless indoors whatever he was wearing. No one after him played the roguish male nearly so well. It is a lost art, and his is probably a lost breed.

If Gable was the prototypical American, the England-born Cary Grant has been the mid-Atlantic, stateless, classless (but very classy), debonair romantic figure, as much at ease in beaneries as in marble halls, moving with wit, assurance, and charm wherever the action takes him. Like Gable, he exerted a strong romantic appeal on women (and still does) without arousing men to anger or contempt. A wider-ranging actor than Gable, Grant has excelled at heroic action (*Gunga Din*) and straight drama (*None But the Lonely Heart*), but most often in exercises of ro-

Stardom's finest hour: Clark Gable as Rhett Butler, Vivien Leigh as Scarlett O'Hara in the only film known by its initials, GWTW.

mantic charm, from *Holiday* to *North by Northwest* and beyond. The dream of a rakish, cosmopolitan, time-defying insouciance may be the most elusive of all the starry dreams, for the men who would possess it as for the women who would be courted by it, Grant, retired but agelessly elegant and dashing in his seventies, remains a unique and uniquely appealing star figure.

In these later, more knowing years, we are all familiar with horror stories about child stars who in fact lost their childhoods to their parents' greedy ambition or who ended up broke, bitter, unbalanced, and even dead because they could not cope with the silence after the cheering stopped. But in the 1930s child stars were the most potent of all, igniting dreams of glory for parents and children alike. Shirley Temple, Mickey Rooney, and Judy Garland really were the neighborhood kids rocketing to lollipop luxury. How much they earned for the tap-dance teachers and voice coaches of the world would probably stagger us all.

Graham Greene, who was writing movie criticism in the late thirties, found unhealthy sexual overtones in the popularity of Shirley Temple. He lost a libel suit for his pains in saying so, and he was probably wrong anyway. Shirley was exceptionally cute, exceptionally quick, exceptionally precocious (even if she was always a year older than Fox said she was). But she was also and primarily the exceptional daughter everybody—or almost everybody—wanted to have, the girl other little girls wanted to be.

The star system, the studio mills, could not in the end create stars. It could straighten their teeth and their noses, style their hair, teach them to walk and speak and perhaps even to act, pose them by the hour in the stills department (the starlets in the Santa Claus bikinis, holding placards imploring us

The legendary romantic star, Humphrey Bogart as a cynical expatriate who puts duty above his love for Ingrid Bergman in Casablanca.

to mail early), get them in the fan magazines, plant them at premieres and store openings, give them walk-ons in two, three, four movies a year (James Stewart appeared in five films in his first year in Hollywood). But ultimately the system could only expose the hopefuls to the possible lightning of acclaim. And the lightning struck only rarely.

Why the lightning strikes, or doesn't, still is an intricate question. Why Lana Turner survived to superstardom while a thousand identically symmetrical young women sagged from sight cannot be explained wholly in terms of luck, roles, a favoring studio executive, a relentless agent, or reams of publicity (some of it vile). What seems to emerge between the press-agentry and the calculated imageries of glamour is the audience's hunch that Lana Turner is not a goddess but a woman—maybe not Miss IQ of 1940, but spontaneous, likable, sexy, and very likely even more of a sucker for a lost romantic cause than you or I. She somehow satisfied wish projections and dreams of escape. The motion-picture camera, like the television camera, seems to have something like x-ray capabilities, the power to perceive qualities of the spirit that viewers respond to, as they did in Lana Turner.

In the 1950s and until her swift, sad, early death in 1962, Marilyn Monroe was perhaps the supreme example of the star whose appeal resided in her interior qualities far more than she seemed to realize. Fox gave her a clever and careful build-up, and she was undeniably and irresistibly beautiful, sexy, individual, piquant, and amusing. But there was more to her than that—an upsetting aspiration to get beyond the sex-kitten imagery, a frightened vulnerability combined with a quirky defensiveness, both growing out of an erratic and disturbing early life compounded by her chattel-like status as a hot Hollywood property.

Multiple Marilyns in How to Marry a Millionaire *show the sex symbol she was for an entire generation—an image she finally found unbearable.*

Her tragedy seemed, after the fact, to be that she did not fully comprehend how much the public cared about her or that it saw her not merely as a sex symbol but as a beautiful and particular actress. She didn't know her own real and time-defying strength, and no one told her in time.

Even as Marilyn Monroe was dying, the star system of which she had been one of the last triumphs was itself dying, an early casualty of all the revolutionary changes that began for Hollywood with the end of World War II.

In the face of the steadily rising postwar income taxes, the superstars could no longer afford to stay on straight studio contracts, which meant that their salaries were fully taxable. More and more of them left studio rosters to work on a free-lance basis, becoming corporations for which they were themselves the principal assets. James Stewart, arriving home from the Air Force, led the parade into the new corporate day, in quest of capital gains instead of astronomical studio salaries.

As it happened, the separation of stars from studios was inevitable. The studios, cutting production and costs in the face of shrinking attendance and declining revenues, could no longer afford massive overheads (swollen during the fat war years), of which actors' salaries were a large percentage.

"My father," Richard Zanuck said wistfully one day during his own tenure as head of production at Twentieth Century-Fox, which Darryl Zanuck had guided through its richest years, "could cast any movie he wanted to make from the list of names on a sheet of paper he kept under the glass top of his desk." By the son's day, the Fox company of players—headed by Tyrone Power, Betty Grable, Don Ameche, Henry Fonda, and Carmen Miranda among many others—was long dispersed. The famous Little Red Schoolhouse on the lot, where Shirley Temple and a generation of young Fox players had studied, had

been shut down years before. Fox had multiple-picture deals with several stars, but exclusive contracts with none.

By the mid-1960s MGM, which for so long had had the largest and best stable of players in the industry, had only one contract actor left, an engaging young man now active in television, Chad Everett.

The star system survives today only at Universal, which alone among the majors still vigorously looks for potential star material, signs performers to exclusive contracts, grooms them, and seeks to build them up to stardom. Universal's large schedule of television production is the contemporary equivalent of the B picture of former times: showcases for new faces. Valerie Perrine is the newest of Universal's contract players to win conspicuous success, first as Montana Wildhack in *Slaughterhouse-Five* (1972), then as Honey Bruce in *Lenny* (1974). Katharine Ross was a Universal player on loan to Avco-Embassy when she made her impressive appearance in *The Graduate* in 1967.

It began to seem possible in the 1960s that the *idea* of the star might be a postwar casualty, along with the studio star system. The alarms (or the cheers) proved to be premature: the success of Redford and Newman in a sleek, lightweight entertainment (*The Sting*) left no doubt that in box-office terms there was still no substitute for the presence of stars riding in the appropriate vehicle. *The Towering Inferno* in 1974, with all its pyrotechnical splendors, would probably have done well with lesser faces, but Newman and Steve McQueen in the major roles (and the likes of Fred Astaire, Jennifer Jones, and O. J. Simpson in supporting roles) unquestionably added to the film's incandescence, and its grosses.

The decline of the star system was reported prematurely. For better and also for worse, it is still alive and reinvigorated by several factors, of which the most obvious is simply

Larger than life, Charlton Heston has specialized in heroic figures, as in the spectacle Ben Hur, *often obscuring his acting gifts for quieter roles.*

that star names help a successful film do even better at the box office. What is also true is that the present generation of studio executives, uncertain of their own taste and judgment and even less certain of the audience's, buy star names as insurance, hedges against disaster, lines of defense against boards of directors demanding to know (later) why a film failed. Well, it didn't fail for lack of trying, fellows: we had Star X and paid him a million bucks plus a percentage of the gross profits, if there'd been any.

The theater owners have probably been the strongest force in keeping the star system alive. They can't put unknown names on their marquees, and there is some evidence that the exhibitors would rather have a poor picture with good names than a great picture with no names. And because the number of play dates a movie can get is crucial to its earning power, the push is to hire a star name or two or three that the theater men can recognize, even if the casting makes no sense and may compromise the strength of the story.

By the mid-70s, the pressure to have star castings, combined with a severe shortage of agreed stars, had led to a grotesque inflation of salaries for the lucky few. Most producers agree with Herb Jaffe (who did *The Wind and The Lion* in 1975) that there are no more than a golden dozen male superstars, whose commitment to a project ensures that it will be financed and made. There are perhaps two women, Barbra Streisand and Elizabeth Taylor, and even they could not absolutely ensure the filming of a particular project.

"But," producer Jaffe said one day at lunch, "if Bob Redford would commit to make it, I could get *this* financed"—and he held up the restaurant's menu.

So it is that Marlon Brando and Jack Nicholson were paid $1,250,000 each for six to eight weeks of work on *The Missouri Breaks* and Steve McQueen was reportedly offered

Gene Hackman went from a supporting role in the film Bonnie and Clyde *to star parts in* French Connection *and (here)* Lucky Lady.

(but rejected) $3,000,000 to appear in Francis Ford Coppola's *Apocalypse Now!* and Charles Bronson now regularly commands a million dollars-plus for each film.

It is pleasant for the stars but unhealthy for the movies as a form of art because escalating costs breed timidity and compromise. Star salaries, doubling and trebling the cost of a movie, discourage the use of original or offbeat material and increase the chances that the movie will fail to make a profit.

The hard truth is that star names do not automatically guarantee box-office bonanzas. Burt Reynolds is one of the most colorful of a new generation of stars and he has been featured in a succession of money-spinners like *White Lightning* and *The Longest Yard* (both 1975) and *Gator* (1976). But he could not save Peter Bogdanovich's musical *At Long Last Love* (1975) from fiscal disaster, nor could Reynolds, Liza Minnelli, and Gene Hackman (stars all) prevent *Lucky Lady* (1976) from being an $11,000,000 flop. There is at least one heavy loser in the record of virtually every surviving superstar: *Number One* (1969) for Charlton Heston, *The Parallax View* (1971) for Warren Beatty, Mike Nichols's *The Fortune* (1975) for both Beatty and Nicholson, Robert Altman's *Buffalo Bill and the Indians* for Paul Newman, and so on.

The rise of television brought about the fall of filmgoing as a habit and created a new audience, more severe and testing than most critics, whose members no longer automatically go to anything, stars or no stars. The customers are selective, attending only the movie the star will improve and not merely adorn. The primacy of the material, the script, has become total. The stars, as in astrology, cannot compel; they may impel, abetting a right cause. The importance of the material and the sharp selectivity of present audiences have made stardom a chancy and elusive state.

Burt Reynolds, who always seems better than the roles he gets, had one of his best as a rugged footballer in The Longest Yard.

Although she has done lovely work since, notably as the shared lady in the lives of Butch Cassidy and the Sundance Kid, Katharine Ross (and Universal) found nothing to equal or extend her scintillating success in *The Graduate*. Jon Voigt after *Midnight Cowboy*, Elliott Gould and Donald Sutherland after *M*A*S*H*, Peter Fonda and Dennis Hopper after *Easy Rider* are a handful of the sizable company of performers who have found success intermittent and those initial triumphs hard to repeat on the same scale.

The sharp shrinkage in the number of movies made has made stardom hard to find and harder to sustain. Then, too, stardom is not quite the same thing: the rules have changed. Each generation rather subtly alters the specifications for its stars, reflecting new currents and aspirations in the society at large. These revised specifications, and what they say

Tough-minded and talented, Barbra Streisand has been one of the very few female superstars to come along since Elizabeth Taylor.

Charles Bronson, Clint Eastwood, Charlton Heston, Dustin Hoffman, Jack Lemmon, and Lee Marvin, and, internationally, Sean Connery, Michael Caine, and Roger Moore exist as male superstars in the charismatic tradition. Marlon Brando, the actor most admired by the actors of any generation, occupies a special place in the literature of stardom. So does John Wayne, whose career is now into its second half-century, and so in a greatly different way does Woody Allen. Coming along strongly, but dependent still on a fortunate succession of roles, are Al Pacino, Robert DeNiro, Richard Dreyfuss, and the latest arrival, Sylvester Stallone, the author-star of *Rocky*, a rousing hit at the end of 1976.

What is to be noted is that each is a skilled actor, with an appeal that does not rest exclusively on old-fashioned romantic allure.

McQueen has done his best work as a working-class, blue-collar hero, or perhaps more precisely as a well-defined character with a capacity for heroism. His fire chief in *The Towering Inferno* lent dignity to an exploitation epic.

Newman's blue-eyed Adonis good looks sometimes seem to work against his high seriousness and rich gifts as an actor, but his performance as the coldly selfish and destructive title figure in *Hud* (1963) is unforgettable.

Like Newman, Redford is romantically handsome (and found his first large following in a romantic comedy, *Barefoot in the Park* with Jane Fonda in 1967), but he is able to play ambiguous and even dubious figures, like the icy and self-centered skier in *Downhill Racer* (1969) and the weak and self-protecting writer married to Streisand in *The Way We Were* (1973).

Warren Beatty, an even more glamorous personality off-screen than on, has in his best work—in Arthur Penn's *Mickey One* (1965) and *Bonnie and Clyde* (1967) and in his own *Shampoo* (1975)—consistently been a very

about society, show up interestingly in a new generation of movie men and women who are more than just a string of pretty faces.

Considering just the men first: Steve McQueen, Paul Newman, Robert Redford, Warren Beatty, Jack Nicholson, Burt Reynolds,

The man of action and not many words, Clint Eastwood found stardom in Italian westerns after a so-so early career at home.

modern man, pushed and tugged by a society he can only respond to. As the swinging hair stylist in *Shampoo,* he was essentially too passive to be an antihero, let alone a hero, and he offered a character to be thought about rather than felt for.

The enormously versatile Nicholson, visible in 1975 in roles as diverse as the neurotic journalist in Antonioni's *The Passenger* and as a vacant-eyed comical dimwit in *The Fortune,* has like Dustin Hoffman reversed Hollywood tradition, progressing from character actor to superstar. After *The Graduate* Hoffman retained a following with intense and involving portrayals of characters, like Ratso in *Mid-*

night Cowboy, at the ragged edges of sanity and survival.

Reynolds, who has been more effective as a rascally antihero, cutting a swath through the lower middle class with forays into the satiny boudoirs of the rich, has a flair for light comedy that ironically has shown up most effectively only on late-night television and in a self-mocking cameo in Mel Brooks' *Silent Movie* (1976). To date, Reynolds is a superstar who has yet to find the perfect role.

Both Clint Eastwood and Charles Bronson had to go abroad to make it as American stars. Bronson, who came out of the Pennsylvania mining country and found his way to the Pasadena Playhouse, was a moderately busy actor in movies and television until European producers discovered that his stern-faced and faintly menacing inscrutability was potent stuff at the international box office. Having left as a character actor, he returned as an authentic million-dollar star, an experienced actor who will outlast the macho casting. Eastwood, one of the few television series stars to transfer to major movie stardom, did it through a series of Italian westerns commencing with *A Fistful of Dollars* in 1964, invariably playing a mysterious, ruthless, remorseless, and virtually wordless wanderer. Those roles, and the roles back home, in hyper-violent detective fare like *Dirty Harry* (1971), have been more demanding physically than histrionically; but Eastwood's craft and assurance before the camera are, like John Wayne's, easy to underestimate, and his image of rugged likable individualism make him Wayne's closest heir apparent.

In a time of stars who began as actors, Heston recalls an earlier time when actors began as stars. Still frequently cast in roles that demand heroics rather than subtleties, Heston has had to take to the stage to remind the world that he can be a wide-ranging actor. The opportunities in the movies—*Will Penny*

The two old pros, John Wayne, a star for 50 years, and James Stewart, in movies since 1935, appeared together in The Shootist.

(1968) in which he played a tramp cowboy was one—have been scarce.

Jack Lemmon made an early career of playing young, amusing, and bumbling Everymen, innocents not quite equipped to handle the world but saved from disaster by his very innocence. Later he explored the dark territories where nice guys can get lost, as when the pressures of the business world erode idealism and hope in *Save the Tiger* (1973).

Lee Marvin had the mixed luck to create a character—the drunken cowboy in 1965's *Cat Ballou*—so indelible that some of his later work, mumbling and extravagant, has seemed to be Marvin mocking Marvin. Then again, a large part of his appeal as a star is that the audience perceives his own extravagant, unconventional, and even self-damaging gusto.

Of the English-speaking stars from abroad, Michael Caine is probably the most versatile screen actor, proved by his ability to hold his own opposite the magical and formidable Laurence Olivier in *Sleuth* (1972). His portrait of the coolly uncommitting womanizer Alfie remains a stunning piece of acting, and although Caine in the years since has appeared in a flood of trashy pictures simply to keep working, he has done memorable work, as in the little-seen but harshly impressive *Get Carter* (1971), about English gangsterism.

Caine, and indeed Sean Connery and Roger Moore, are followers in the Cary Grant tradition of the debonair and classless Englishman at home equally in palaces or truckers' cafes, with traces of non-U accents, Cockney or Glaswegian, opening doors that would stay closed to the plummy tones of Oxford and the BBC. Moore, handsome in the matinee idol mold, shows signs of moving from the arch sophistication of the Saint to a rumpled and bawdy charm that is nearer to his own muscular personality. Connery, freed by his own efforts from his strong but limiting image as the first and most popular James Bond, was

An international star, Michael Caine won an Oscar nomination for his role as a Cockney swinger in Alfie *in 1966.*

Lovers at twilight, Sean Connery and Audrey Hepburn were a middle-aged Robin and Marian *in her first film in nearly a decade.*

a fine actor long before 007 (in Sidney Lumet's *The Hill* back in 1965 most notably) and now proves consistently—*Robin and Marian* opposite Audrey Hepburn in 1976 was a good example—that he is a warmly sympathetic and competent actor-star.

The origins of both Connery and Caine are deep in the working class, and there seems little doubt that, like the stars of the Hollywood thirties, they exist as envied and admired symbols of escape from the gray tediums of borderline solvency.

In the newest American generation, Al Pacino and Robert DeNiro, both seen to be strong and almost obsessively private men and dedicated actors, have had the good fortune of important roles they could make the most of. It is clear that, like Hoffman, they prefer to be star-actors rather than stars. In either guise, they are certain to be steadily conspicuous.

Since his debut in the late 1950s, Sidney Poitier had stood alone as the only nonsinging, nondancing black male superstar. But the discovery by the movies in the 1970s of a distinct, reachable, and lucrative black audience led not only to a rush of black movies but to the creation of an entire new population of black writers, directors, producers, actors, and stars. By now Poitier has been joined in the top rank by James Earl Jones, Billy Dee Williams, Fred Williamson, Jim Brown, O. J. Simpson, Raymond St. Jacques, and Richard Roundtree (who played Shaft). All of them, and others on the next lower rung, appear to have the talent and the appeal to reach the whole audience rather than the black audience only and most already have. Indeed, the trends in film move so swiftly that the black film for black audiences has already given way to the so-called crossover film consciously aimed at the entire audience; and the violent "blacksploitation" films, usually about the criminal aspects of the black ghettos, have yielded to films that begin to explore the whole range of black life in America.

There are fewer female stars than there have ever been. Like the men, those who can fairly be called stars are apt to be intelligent, skilled, and experienced actresses first, beautiful more often than not, but rarely only splendid to look upon. For the women success is even harder to sustain than for the men, which is understandable because there continue to be so few major roles for women. Those women who do survive and succeed are in significant ways different from the elegant and pedestaled stars of the Golden Age, sharing (and resolutely insisting upon) mobility, independence, self-determination. Perhaps because foreign films reflected life in a more realistic way earlier than Hollywood was able to, an electrifying new breed of actresses came to the foreground first in Europe.

There was Sophia Loren at the top of a whole class of vibrant Italian actresses. There were Jeanne Moreau and Simone Signoret from France and Melina Mercouri from Greece. Most particularly there was an entire generation of English performers: Julie Christie, Vanessa and Lynn Redgrave, Maggie Smith, Glenda Jackson, Susan Hampshire, Jacqueline Bisset, and Sarah Miles. In Sweden, Ingmar Bergman produced a company of superlative actresses all by himself: Ingrid Thulin, Harriett Andersson, Bibi Andersson, Liv Ulmann.

Most were startlingly beautiful, but it was abundantly clear that there were special and shared traits of character that gave them their extraordinary appeal. They were, one knew and one saw, honest-to-God women, not mannequins, and they exulted in being independent, although they had also suffered for their vulnerabilities as women in love. Their charm and attractiveness—for both the men and women in the audience, but especially for the women—lay in the widely understood truth of their fierce and uncompromising zest for personal expression and mobility. They were liberated, and were acknowledged as liberated, even before the women's movement had been codified and organized. In a computerized world in which we all feel, in the words of Ulysses S. Grant, tethered by the iron chain of circumstance, these women defied the tethers—except when they chose not to, and even then it was on their own terms.

At that, the new generation of women in film reflected more than the growing restlessness and resentments of women in society. They reflected a more mature understanding among those in the audience of the nature of relationships and the ingredients of romantic attraction (as against the simplistic myths

A new kind of womanly appeal came to Hollywood with Simone Signoret, here in Stanley Kramer's Ship of Fools; *Oskar Werner co-starred.*

Hollywood had been conjuring up for years). Simone Signoret in Stanley Kramer's 1965 *Ship of Fools*—sick, fat, without makeup, perspiring with fear—was a revelation in her sensual appeal and her womanly warmth, even in extremis.

The American director Joseph Losey, now living and working in England, was once discussing the appeal of Jeanne Moreau, whom he directed in an ill-starred venture called *Eve*. "An actress," he said, "has to be a mixture of toughness and vulnerability. If she is too vulnerable she is apt to be destroyed; witness Marilyn. But if she is too tough, she is worthless. Jeanne ricochets from one destructive love affair to another—destructive for her. But when she has to, she can walk over you with hobnail boots, as I can attest." It is just that eagerness to experience, even at the risk of pain, that made Jeanne Moreau so stunning in *Jules and Jim* and her other early films.

Julie Christie as the rootless free spirit of *Billy Liar* (1963) and then the bored darling of *Darling* (1965), dissatisfied but seemingly unable to define who she is or what it is she really wants, is an authentic creation for her time. As recently as *Shampoo*, playing a

Faye Dunaway, a star since Bonnie and Clyde, *has done well as the beauty who is brainy yet neurotic, as in the satire* Network.

woman making compromises with the world to avoid intolerable restrictions on her freedom, she is still portraying a recognizable figure in the modern landscape, with sympathetic vibrations from her own free-floating life.

It has not in general been so fruitful a period for American actresses. Yet Shirley MacLaine has established a domestic tradition of the outspoken, politically concerned and active, convention-defying, many-talented free woman, shaping her life exactly to her own tastes. Jane Fonda, equally talented and even more emphatically outspoken, proclaims the same strong-willed independence (and at greater costs in career terms). Nor are Karen Black, Sally Kellerman, Mia Farrow, and Ali McGraw afraid to turn their backs on traditional standards of propriety.

Faye Dunaway has suffered through some sappy roles since she was Bonnie to Beatty's Clyde, but at her most effective—even as a cartoon of the aggressive career woman in *Network* (1976)—she convincingly portrays the dilemma of the beauty whose brains are thought to be a beastly nuisance and who is driven to the brink by the gap between her aspirations, for love as well as for success, and her possibilities.

While the sense of their private personalities has received less attention from the general public, Gena Rowlands, Ellen Burstyn, Cloris Leachman, Diane Ladd, and Geraldine Page (all candidates for anyone's list of the finest screen actresses of any time) have earned particular admiration for their ability to portray with insight and accuracy contemporary women caught up in the painful and often demoralizing pressures of being women in a society creaking toward change.

The nonconformist spirit among women stars has its counterpart among the men. Marlon Brando straddles the tradition, as icon and iconoclast, a superstar in the majestic old style who is also a rebel with several causes. He remains without serious challenge as the finest film actor of them all, the one most revered by other actors, for reasons made absolutely clear in the tearing despair of his expatriate in *Last Tango in Paris.*

Jack Nicholson, the most recent of the male superstars, is probably the least politically concerned of his fellows, but he honors the tradition of a lively disinterest in the outward trappings of stardom. Like Dustin Hoffman, he is first and last a star-actor who has come

A graying Marlon Brando showed his matchless acting as the grieving expatriate finding brief solace with Maria Schneider in Last Tango in Paris.

a long hard way from the bits and the biker pictures. He is devilishly handsome, but his gift is to play persuasively the edgy modern man, faintly or not so faintly neurotic, whistling and carousing past the graveyard of his hopes. He is a star not only because he embodies that old wistful dream of success but also because he sparks that shock of identification: he is where we are.

There are reasonable laments for the death not of stars but of the studio system that tried to generate stars. Actors now arrive by a harder route, from campuses and regional theaters and repertory companies. But once arrived, they are better prepared, and probably reconciled to the likelihood that stardom, even if they find it, won't be quite what it once was. They may not even much care.

What is important is that a new breed of actors and actresses, closely attuned to their audiences and with strong sympathies for many of the characters they are playing, give the movies an important new means of describing the world as it is—not necessarily tragically, either.

The movies and the surviving stars cannot retrieve the past, but they can help us to comprehend, embrace, and get by in the present.

The toy that grew even faster

In the middle of the 1970s it is very hard to imagine how we could be more thoroughly television-saturated than we are. Statistics compiled by the authoritative trade publication, *Broadcasting* magazine, revealed that at the end of 1974 there were 112 million television sets in use in 68.5 million U.S. households. In other words, television is watched in 97 percent of all American homes (excluding Alaska and Hawaii). The other 3 percent still staring at their radios seem to be an irreducible minimum, a statistic unchanged from the previous year.

While survey samplings are suspect, the A. C. Nielsen organization's estimate is that in the average household in 1974 television was watched for six hours and forty-nine minutes a day. In the course of a week television reached something like 87 percent of everyone in the country beyond the age of seventeen (and a very large slice of those under seventeen as well). Advertisers spent more than $3.5 billion trying to reach the television audience,

which works out to about fifty-one dollars for every household.

From its standing start in 1954, color television inched along until its big breakthrough in 1964, when 1.7 million sets were sold. The following year 3 million sets were sold, a year later 5 million, and the year after that 6.3 million. By now there are more than 43 million color sets in use.

But the most significant new statistic (and the one showing the steepest climb) is the number of home television sets now linked to cable systems. The latest estimate by *Broadcasting* magazine early in 1975 was 12 percent or 8.2 million households, an increase of more than 2 million homes in only a year. By 1980, 60 percent of American households are expected to be cable-linked.

What the cable delivery systems mean for television as a medium is diversity, a deliverance from the tyranny of box-car numbers that spell success or failure for network programming, or indeed for all commercial pro-

Polishing his appellation, Jack Paar, the host who made his late night talk show into a national viewing habit, achieves sidewalk immortality on famous Hollywood Boulevard.

gramming. Cable hookups have already meant new audiences and new life for many of the UHF stations, whose signals without cable are difficult to receive. Cable has been particularly beneficial to educational stations (such as KCET—Channel 28—the Public Broadcasting outlet in Los Angeles) trapped in the UHF ghetto and unable to buy their way into the VHF dial. KCET is now home-delivered by more than fifty different cable systems over a far wider area than a VHF signal covers in Los Angeles and no longer has any real need to try for a VHF channel allocation. Because the last VHF station to come onto the market in Southern California was being offered at $15 million, it is good that the station is not pressed to go to VHF; its limited funds would be better spent on improving its facilities and programming.

Creating audiences for UHF stations is only one function of the cable systems. (They began, in Pennsylvania, as community antennas to provide stronger signals in towns where reception was blocked or impaired. There are now nearly 5,000 cable systems in the United States, more than 900 in Pennsylvania, and nearly 1,000 in California.)

Cable's original function has been expanded. In addition to supplying strong signals on the VHF channels and for most UHF channels, some cable systems have begun offering their own (as yet quite limited) programming. Theta Cable in Los Angeles offers first-run movies, uncut and uninterrupted, on a special channel for an additional monthly fee of about seven dollars. Elsewhere, in two dozen cities from New York to San Diego, firms using leased cable channels offer their customers movies on a pay-as-you-see basis, transmitting or unscrambling the picture only at the request of the viewer. Sooner or later these systems will offer nonlocal commercial channels and satellite showings of new movies, including movies made especially for cable-sys-

Live and non-commercial, the Sesame Street bird greets Los Angeles fans. The popular children's show, a joyful way to learn, has helped public television to widen its following.

tem viewing in the same way they are now made especially for network viewing. The technology already exists by which a single cable hookup could carry nearly eighty signals into a subscriber's living room. The uses that have been projected (or prophesied) include the delivery of telegrams, mail, and even the daily newspaper. The equipment being installed by many cable systems has room for thirty inputs or options, although not all of these are yet in use.

It is clear that the diversification of the television experience has hardly begun. It also seems clear that the quantitative growth of television has surely peaked. The number of two- and three-set households will edge upward (revealing, if nothing else, that the trade-in value of old sets is so inconsequential that one might as well hang on to them). But the latitudinal outreach of television has gone about as far as it can go. We are also near saturation: certainly we are near to being saturated by the mix of television as it has been until now. Proof is found in the increasing instability of network programming, the sudden deaths and quick reshufflings of series, the ever-more-nervous attempts to keep the interest of an audience whose attention span is ever-shortening.

Like the movies in 1946, television has seemingly reached the end of its beginnings. If the motion picture was a toy that grew up, so is television, but television, the living room toy, grew even faster. In fact, television in its quarter of a century (roughly) has gone through most of the same stages it took the movies three-quarters of a century (roughly) to cover. Popular novelty; first exploratory forays into serious programming; growth of mass packaging for a mass audience; maturity within the mass system; diversification into appeals to both mass and minority audiences: television has moved so fast that its relationship to theatrical motion pictures has been changing constantly.

In the beginning it seemed that the movies' best recipe for survival was to do what television could not do as well, or do at all—wider screens, bigger spectacles, bigger stars. It quickly came to mean harder themes, harsher language, more explicit sex and violence, and, much more subtly, a view of the world in which there was irony and ambiguity, poetic injustice as well as virtue triumphant. Let television, the new mass-entertainment medium,

The first Emmy winner—in 1948 when the awards were in Los Angeles only—was Shirley Dinsdale, with her puppet pal Judy Splinters.

be all things to all people, Everyman at his leisure.

And so to those specifications television had begun. Would anyone like to hazard a guess as to who won the first Emmy Award as Most Outstanding Television Personality? The year was 1948, if that helps. It doesn't. She was Shirley Dinsdale, a puppeteer whose character was called Judy Splinters. In the days before the coaxial cable linked the east and west coasts, the Emmys were strictly a

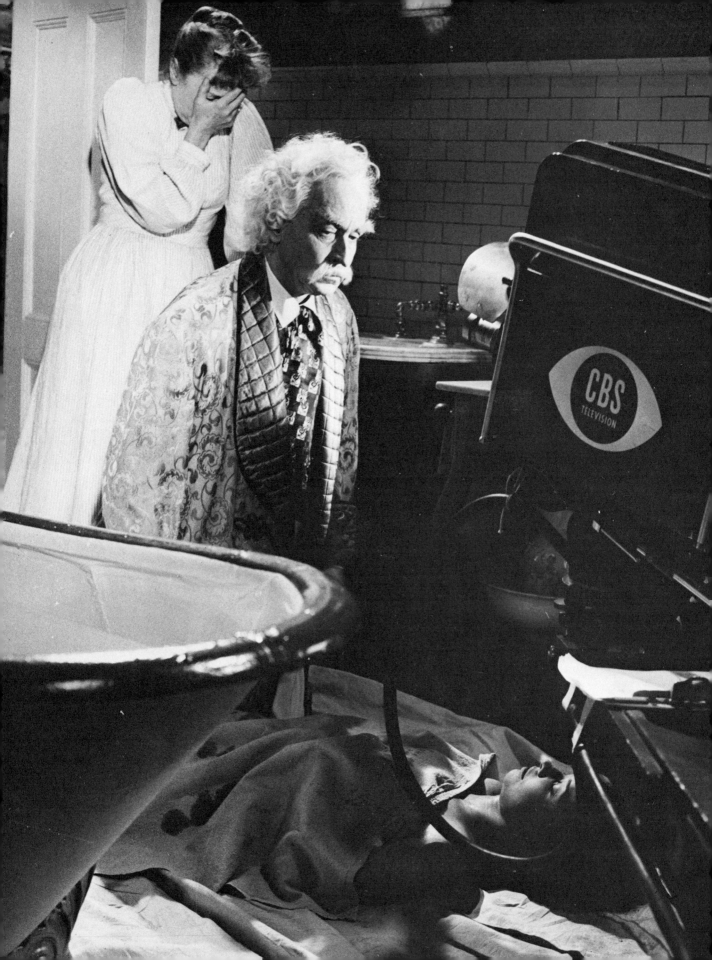

Los Angeles affair. The most popular television show, in those first awards, was "Mike Stokey's Pantomime Quiz."

Those were the novelty days, when television flourished in saloons in the same way as early movies were often sandwiched between the soubrette and the trained rats on vaudeville bills. And if the movies soon found D. W. Griffith, television found live drama and a new generation of writers and directors to make it happen: Reginald Rose and Paddy Chayefsky, Delbert Mann and John Frankenheimer, and many more. In a brief, beautiful flowering in the mid-fifties before the numbers game took over, the dramatic anthology ("live from New York") was a staple of television: "Robert Montgomery Presents," "Studio One," the "U.S. Steel Hour," "Producers' Showcase," "Matinee Theatre" (with incredible *daily* drama), "Ford Star Jubilee," the "Kraft Television Theater," and the most ambitious of them all, "Playhouse 90."

The movies were selling their vaults to television by then, but television was for the first time providing the stuff of movies: Reginald Rose's *Twelve Angry Men,* Rod Serling's *Patterns* and *Requiem for a Heavyweight,* Paddy Chayefsky's *Marty.*

Drama was not the half of it, of course, and there were Alistair Cooke's literate and wide-ranging "Omnibus," the Fred Astaire specials with Barrie Chase, the not-yet-surpassed varieties of Milton Berle, Ed Wynn, Perry Como, Dinah Shore, and Steve Allen, and the astonishing comic richness of the Sid Caesar–Imogene Coca "Your Show of Shows" (which was done live, despite the formidable challenges of its beautifully timed and often very physical sketches).

It was a particular richness, not to be sustained. More and more in the early sixties, television became a series business: "The Defenders," "Ben Casey," "Dr. Kildare," "The Naked City," "Gunsmoke," "Bonanza,"

Drama anthologies like Playhouse 90, *here starring Franchot Tone, were certainly the pride of early television but they lost the rating war.*

Imogene Coca, a fine comedienne, went from the Sid Caesar show to her own brief series, Grindl.

"Hazel," "The Dick Van Dyke Show," "The Beverly Hillbillies." The range was from the abysmal to the sublime, the extremes linked only by a shared week-to-week predictability.

There were marvelous things; there always are. The odd special, usually underwritten by an institutional sponsor more interested in a good image than in good ratings (and with enough clout to force a network to sell it the air time), the public affairs program undertaken at a loss to preserve the license, the major news event, which television reports with such thrilling immediacy and which is its greatest strength. But a space shot, an election night, Carol Burnett and Julie Andrews at Carnegie Hall serve then as now as forceful reminders that commercial television is first and always an advertising medium, fiercely competitive,

but competitive in a quest not for excellence but for the broadcast common denominator, the fattest ratings. There may be no news in that observation, but it is still worth nothing when, after nearly thirty years, no visible sign of significant change can be detected.

In the mid-sixties there was not even yet the promise of the effective alternative that public television has slowly and precariously become. What was still called educational television was worthy, solemn, and dull. The early noncommercial stations clung thinly to life by fulfilling contracts with the public schools, airing daytime classroom materials.

Meanwhile, "Bonanza" was costing $200,000 an episode in 1966, was being syn-

Talk, and quantities of it, still fills television programming; some of the best has been provoked by David Susskind on his Open End.

dicated in eight languages to sixty countries, and had a weekly audience estimated at 350 million viewers. Television, like radio, in its first years had a fair amount of fifteen-minute programming, then shifted to the half-hour and ninty-minute shows. Two-hour programs, of which there were none in 1957, constituted a fifth of network scheduling by 1968.

The lesson of the huge ratings earned by movies on television was not lost on network executives. (*The Bridge on the River Kwai* was calculated to have been watched by an

audience of 60 million on its first television airing. *Gone with the Wind* was seen by an estimated 90 million in its first network appearance late in 1976.) The first movies specifically made for television were produced in 1965, and in the decade since several hundred have been made, fulfilling Sam Goldwyn's prophecy of the mid-forties that Hollywood would work for television.

Movies for television have in the best and worse senses become the B movies of our time. They are made with ruthless efficiency, on budgets that rarely exceed $1 million and are often considerably less, on shooting schedules twice and even three times faster than for a theatrical feature of the same length.

One of the medium's biggest stars, in every way, was Jackie Gleason, who mixed clever comedy and fancy trimmings, and retired in comfort.

They are a testing ground for new talent. They are heavier on plot than characterization, and the plot conveniently breaks into as many acts as there are commercial breaks. They are shot with the smaller screen in mind, revealed in the number of close-ups and medium-distance shots.

Like the movies that used to serve as the bottom half of double features, the best of the movies made for television have very positive qualities. They have energy and pace and a lack of pretension. Emotions run strong and

Television's reigning royalty (overleaf) *after all these years are still Bob Hope and Lucille Ball, here teamed for a special.*

A clown prince, Red Skelton and his zany characters, including here blond-fancying Clem Kadiddlehopper, had a long and endearing TV run.

mental melodrama starring James Caan as a doomed pro-football player in a story drawn from life, failed at the box office, although it was offered at a reduced price. Obviously a movie that has been presented free in the living room must have a special claim on the attentions of the audience before people will go out and spend money to see it again. It happens, although not on a major scale, with classic movies that have been shown on television. Indeed, the frequent TV appearances of *Citizen Kane*, *Casablanca*, and other imperishable film favorites seem to have stimulated rather than diminished interest in seeing them in theaters. A film-lover can work up a desire bordering on obsession to see his favorites unbutchered, uninterrupted, and fullsize.

But to see even a superior movie made for television under theatrical conditions is an oddly revealing experience. It suffers from enlargement, as if a specific density that was quite adequate for the twenty-one-inch screen had gone pale and watery, like bad soup. The intimacy evaporates and the emotional intensity thins like rising smoke. In *Brian's Song* the brusque affection between Caan and his closest football pal, understated and touching on the small screen, looked corny and overstated in the theater.

But it worked in the medium for which it was made, and that is all that really mattered. The point remains that television movies and theatrical movies are not the same. There remains a crucial difference in what, for want of a more precise term, might be called their specific gravity.

It is curious and significant that few of commercial television's most super superstars have subsequently been successful in films. Lucille Ball went the other way, achieving far greater fame, fortune, and longevity in television than she ever could have hoped to have in the movies, where she got her start. Mary

clear (if not pure); endings are decisive and along the way there is likely to have been plenty of atmosphere.

Some of these films have been shown in theaters abroad, and successfully. *Duel*, an extremely well-made truck-chase thriller starring Dennis Weaver, is said to have grossed something like $7 million overseas—and was made for less than $500,000.

A few television movies have been shown in theaters in this country, but without success. Even *Brian's Song*, a very popular senti-

196

Comedy with an edge, sometimes too sharp for the cautious air, has always been the specialty of the Smothers Brothers, Tommy and Dick.

Tyler Moore also began in films (X-15 in 1961), but her story really only starts as Dick Van Dyke's wife on the old "Dick Van Dyke Show," the platform from which she launched her own show (and then a whole television production empire that may finally be more successful than Desilu). But neither she nor Van Dyke has had much luck in the movies. *Mary Poppins* was a runaway hit, and Van Dyke was engaging in it, but it was Julie Andrews's film, and so was *Thoroughly Modern Millie*, in which Mary Tyler Moore was similarly engaging.

Steve McQueen is sometimes cited as a television creation (he did "Wanted Dead or Alive" in 1958), but he was established in films before the series and, although he would prefer it be forgotten, it was *The Blob* that made him famous, in that same year.

Television has not (or not yet) been a proving ground for future film stars. It *has* provided them with work, however, and Robert Redford, unknown and unstarred, shows up in reruns of "The Untouchables" as a sneering, baby-faced killer in one episode. But his career was launched by *Barefoot in the Park*, on Broadway. Sid Caesar's efforts in the movies have, through no lack of his own talent, been embarrassments to everyone who knows how deeply gifted he is. Richard Chamberlain has by now asserted himself as a star actor in films. Yet after his boyish fame as Dr. Kildare he in a real sense started all over again, doing stage work in repertory in England and coming into the movies as the experienced and versatile performer he is, rather than as a television personage.

The failure of transference works both ways, and James Stewart is one film star who has come to sad and sudden termination on television, as have Shirley MacLaine and Tony Curtis, among others.

What all this proves is not quite clear, but I think it is that, in spite of the fact that television and the movies are both visual mediums, they are divided more than they are united by the common language of visual images. "Divided as we are by a common language," George Bernard Shaw said of the English and the Americans, the large public screen and the small private screen are similarly divided. It is a mischief to presume that they are identical, to presume, for example, that theaters have no future because there are movies on television and may be more yet.

Not only are the two forms distinct, but the relationship between them is always in change. By now, most particularly, it is no longer true that the movies' recipe for survival is to do what television can't do as well or do at all, and it is no longer true that television is exclusively Everyman at his leisure.

For their part, the movies, having had a brief but frequently impressive flirtation with social realism, are quickly retreating to the safety of "pure" entertainment, sleek and untroubling escapist offerings of which *The Sting* is the founding model. The movies are not wrong, either, however much they may disappoint admirers who are eager to see the medium do something more than tap dance. But with the real world furnished wall to wall with exacerbations and psychic pain—with problems of energy, employment, recession,

The clean-cut young star, Richard Chamberlain as Dr. Kildare helped to make this series a long-running hit and left him well off but unhappy.

A bearded Chamberlain, after years on stage, returned to television as a versatile actor—here with John Carradine in The Lady's Not For Burning.

scandal, inflation, confrontations in the Middle East and Southeast Asia, and a loss of confidence everywhere—it is no wonder that the customers set forth to be diverted, if they set forth at all.

For its part, television finds that diversion is not quite enough. A diet of sodas may satisfy most of the customers, but not a vocal minority of private citizens, legislators, and government administrators. They have not forgotten Newton Minow's denunciation of television as a cultural wasteland, and they have not seen any genuinely effective reclamation project change the medium since.

So, amongst the Kojaks, television in the middle seventies has occasionally found its voice for expressing social truth in dramatic terms. Tom Gries's *The Migrants*, based on an early short story by Tennessee Williams and starring Cloris Leachman as the gaunt and wiry matriarch of an itinerant brood of crop pickers, was as strongly angry in its way as *The Grapes of Wrath*. It was perhaps all the more effective because it found exploitation and hand-to-mouth existences in a period of national affluence, not depression. The story and its treatment were compassionate but unsentimental, and if its young protagonist finally escaped the endless trap of the migrations, it was only to face more trials, of a different sort, as an unskilled laborer in a cold city. You could not imagine the film succeeding at the motion-picture box office (although it was very well received at the Cannes Festival in 1974 and has been considered for release in Europe). But, produced on a rigorous budget, it worked within the economics of television.

The Autobiography of Miss Jane Pittman, scripted by Tracy Keenan Wynn and directed by John Korty, had as its center a tour de force performance by Cicely Tyson covering an age span of eighty years or more. It also built to a climax of unabashed sentimental

Social realism returned in strong films made for television like Tom Gries' The Migrants, *about the life and hard times of a crop-picking family.*

Defying the laws of segregation provided a moving climax to The Autobiography of Miss Jane Pittman, *which symbolized an entire century of the black experience in America through the life of one woman, stunningly played by Cicely Tyson.*

melodrama, but along the way it looked unevasively at the realities of black history in America, and it did not say that all those woes were behind us.

More controversial than either, because we are still very uptight about treating sex seriously, was *That Certain Summer,* a careful but courageous drama about a teenage boy who discovers during a holiday visit that his divorced father is a homosexual. There were calm, civilized performances by Hal Holbrook and Scott Jacoby as father and son and by Martin Sheen as the father's new partner. They gave the production and story by Richard Levinson and William Link a quiet and in fact almost unemotional dignity. The program proved that important but exploitable material could be handled thoughtfully and nonexploitively.

The Missiles of October was the best of a relatively new television form that its makers called the docu-drama, history as documentary-like drama, fast-moving, and with some eerily accurate impersonations of John Kennedy, Dean Acheson, and other public figures.

Not the least of the forces making for change in commercial television is that there is now an alternative to measure it against. Although public television remains an underfinanced distant cousin, it has, after many a trial, emerged as a fourth network with its share of very palpable hits.

Ironically, it took a British import to make public television a viable alternative and redeem it from its standard fare of two figures talking to each other over a prop coffee table. The BBC's "Forsyte Saga" proved to be the addicting delight here that it has been everywhere else in the world. It brought new viewers and new contributions to the stations and served as a lure for the other programs public television had to offer. The resulting variety was refreshing, including Julia Child,

A new form of television, the docu-drama restages history with actors, as in The Missiles of October, *about the Cuban crisis, with Martin Sheen and William Devane as the Kennedys and Howard da Silva as Premier Krushchev.*

the dazzling "Sesame Street" (modeled in its sophistication and rapid pace after "Laugh-In," which surveys indicated kids watched all the time), the often outspoken works on "Hollywood Television Theater," and a surprisingly wide assortment of music, drama, and classic films from the silent era to the present.

Public television may be healthier if it stays under some financial strain. As in most eleemosynary institutions, a little prosperity goes a long way toward bureaucracy, and public television fights best with its back to the wall, where ingenuity is its prime resource. But the antipathy of the Nixon Administration media baiters, fearing a fourth network because they already were having enough trouble with the three commercial networks, created a bit too much financial strain for public television and left a temporary mark, in the scarcity of public-events programming. Thus PBS stations must have had a deep feeling of satisfaction in presenting their viewers with every damaging word of the Watergate hearings.

The strength of British television has been the dynamic tension between the noncommercial, independent, and richly funded BBC and commercial programmers. The BBC lost three-quarters of its audience when commercial television began, but fought its way back to roughly equal shares. In oversimplified terms, the threat of the commercial channels keeps the BBC from growing too worthily dull, but the existence of the BBC prevents commercial television from becoming too cravenly pop. (On one memorable evening when I was living in London, the commercial channel, testifying to its love of all things cultural, was presenting Katina Paxinou and the Greek National Theater—in Greek, without subtitles. The BBC, yielding to no one in its affection for the common man, was presenting wrestling from Manchester. The wrestling won, with the highest ratings such a show had ever had.)

The dynamic tension in the United States between public and commercial television is David vs. Goliath, and David's sling needs repairs. Although it is a lopsided encounter, it is more interesting and productive than it used to be. If we are lucky, public television will remind us more effectively all along the way of just what television can and ought to do. Commercial television, whose claims of operating in the public interest are coming under sharper scrutiny than they once did, will be harder put to ignore the example of public television.

The Archie Bunkers with their wraths and hang-ups humorously mirror present-day lower-middle-class America on All in the Family, *starring Carroll O'Connor as the prejudiced but persuadable patriarch.*

The birth of television was for the movies both devastating and liberating. The movies were forced but also enabled to seek out new audiences and to explore all the possibilities of the form.

Television faces no such revolutionary occurrence in technologies--no feelies, no shapies, at least not yet. But it is clear that in a slightly less drastic way, television is faced with contending developments that will be liberating if they are not quite devastating.

Cable television is, as noted, growing fast and challenging the hegemony of the three commercial networks and the independent commercial channels.

Although they still retail at the better part of $2,000, an increasing number of television cassette recorders and players like the Sony Betamax are in use, providing yet another alternative in home entertainment.

And there are now two competing systems for recording television images and sound on discs that can be played back through TV sets. One of these, the Phillips-MCA Videodisc system, is very near to market readiness, with the player estimated to cost about $500, the albums from $2 to $10. The systems will further augment the home entertainment complex by providing a new outlet for classic movies—MCA will offer its own, including *Airport, Spartacus,* and *Torn Curtain*—and classic television.

Still the discs do not represent a fundamental shift, only an advance. It is surely cable television that will ultimately have the liberating effect on television that television had on the movies, freeing it to develop all of its possibilities, enabling it to serve the minorities within the mass. If the movies' new day was painful for the old-line major studios, television's new day will be painful for the three major commercial networks. They already are sharing the audience not only with independent commercial stations but increasingly with public TV stations and with the cable channels and their movies-for-pay. Eventually they will have to compete with additional alternatives as yet undreamed of. The networks will not be dethroned as the principal carriers of a mass medium, but that medium will eventually offer as wide an array of choices as the movies do now.

The Bellamys (above) with their faithful servants (below) mirror Edwardian times in public television's successful Upstairs, Downstairs.

Movies, morality, and mischief

There are those who hate and fear what they imagine to be the corrupting power of the movies and who, if they could, would legislate the movies back to the world of Andy Hardy, with its moral certainties, its nice reticences, and its mandatory optimism.

This collective reactive voice was heard loud and angry in California a few years ago from the forces who introduced and fought for an anti-obscenity ballot initiative, Proposition 18. The amendment was solidly rejected by the voters, but the attempt is sure to be made again by those who are convinced that the movies are weakening our moral fiber and leading the nation down a primrose path toward permissiveness, debauchery, violence, and self-indulgence. And toward socialism and communism, some of the movie haters would quickly add, for the fears about what the movies are doing to us morally are often closely linked to fears about what the movies may be trying to do to us politically.

It would be hard to conceive of a more fervently patriotic group than the founding fathers of Hollywood, dedicated as they were to unabashed free enterprise and the American way of life that had done so much for them. The fact that some of them were Jewish immigrants who had made good in a new industry was a source of pride but also some uneasiness and, in a country that was free of pogroms but not of anti-semitism, they declared and demonstrated their Americanism very forcefully. Their private politics were most often Republican, although they enjoyed being on good terms with whichever administration was in power. But the politics that got onto the screen never really went beyond a nondenominational patriotic zeal. Crooked politicians might be a staple of melodrama, but the party label was blurred beyond deciphering and the state depicted was usually geographically situated east of Maine, south of Louisiana, or west of Hawaii.

Up a tree in the altogether, Alan Arkin makes his (and the movie's) protest against the idiocies of war in Mike Nichols' film of Catch-22.

208

An industry trying to be all things to all people was more interested in consensus than argument. The American political process manages to be captivating even when it is dull, as television proves all the time, but politics were always thought to be box-office poison, and generally they were.

The movies warned (dramatically but not really controversially) about the menace of Nazi Germany and Fascist Italy, and during World War II Hollywood put itself totally at the country's service. Even those films that acknowledged problems in the society, like *The Grapes of Wrath* (1940), found grounds for hope and optimism (and history vindicated the ringing optimism Darryl F. Zanuck himself wrote into the last scene of *The Grapes of Wrath*).

Accordingly there was a bitter irony when in 1947 the Un-American Activities Committee of the House of Representatives (HUAC) began to focus its attention on suspected communist infiltration in Hollywood, along with the Broadway stage and the then-infant television industry, centered in New York City. The hearings turned up a number of writers, directors, and performers who were politically left-wing, and a smaller number who were or had been Communist Party members. But what the hearings also confirmed was that the studio system was an almost perfect filter against political ideas of any kind, let alone any ideas of true subversive advocacy.

But thirty years later some of the wounds caused by the HUAC hearings have not yet healed. The economic pressures brought by the studios to induce witnesses to recant or to inform, to name names of those known or thought to be involved in the Party or in other left-wing activities, divided friend from friend, and the sense of betrayal is still fresh. The cooperative witnesses—the late Robert Taylor, Elia Kazan, Budd Schulberg, Clifford Odets among them—gave names if they had

them, sometimes eagerly, more often with visible anguish.

The famous "Unfriendly Ten" writers, directors, and producers went to jail for refusing to testify. (One of them became a jailmate of the chairman of the HUAC, the late J. Parnell Thomas, who was subsequently convicted of tax fraud.) Some among the Ten never worked in the industry again. Others, including the late Dalton Trumbo, Waldo Salt (who adapted *Midnight Cowboy* and *Day of the Locust*), and Ring Lardner, Jr. (*M*A*S*H*) were able to resume their careers, but only after long and costly periods of unemployment or of cut-rate work done anonymously. Only a few months before he died in 1976, Trumbo was given the Oscar he won as "Robert Rich" for *The Brave One* in 1956.

A blacklist, estimated by another of the Ten, Adrian Scott, to have contained more than 200 film-industry names, blighted several careers and remained in force through the 1950s. A similar blacklist existed in television, and even now there are performers whose names are anathema to some sponsors.

It is a measure of a different day that movies and television are able to deal with the period that, as Trumbo later said, had no victors, only victims, and that left no one involved in it unstained by its evil. *Fear on Trial*, a docu-drama on CBS, told the story of John Henry Faulk and his long but successful libel suit against CBS and the blacklist that kept him from performing for a decade.

Martin Ritt's film *The Front* in 1976 was a thinly fictionalized story of the television days in New York in the early 1950s, when private vigilante groups like Aware, Inc., and Red Channels supplemented the pursuits of the HUAC and "cleared" or blacklisted writers and performers for the networks, which caved in under the pressure. Blacklisted writers submitted scripts in the names of front men like the one portrayed by Woody Allen

Making sport of a recent ugly period, The Front *used Zero Mostel and Woody Allen to sharpen its satire on the blacklisting of television writers in the 50s.*

in the film, written by Walter Bernstein. *The Front* was a sweet vindication because, as the closing credits revealed, Ritt, Bernstein, co-star Zero Mostel, and some of the supporting actors had all been blacklisted at the time.

The lingering legacy of the period was a chronic inhibition in the political content of American films, as most significantly reflected in the reluctance of American movies to deal with the Vietnam War, with or without taking sides. The social-realist films of the sixties began to explore problems and shortcomings in the country—drugs, the counterculture of the alienated young, the frustrations in the black ghettos—and the unvarnished truth was seen to be startling, but even here there was little partisanship or advocacy of political action. Instead these movies reflect a cynical disaffection with all politics, which became pervasive following the assassinations of John and Robert Kennedy and Martin Luther King, Jr.

Executive Action, a political melodrama heavily written by Dalton Trumbo in 1974, sought to prove (in fictional terms) the likelihood of a conspiracy in the John Kennedy assassination. A far better film, Alan Pakula's *The Parallax View*, also in 1974, with Warren Beatty as an investigative reporter, tried to demonstrate the theoretical possibility of a

conspiracy that could go undetected despite the inquiries of something like the Warren Commission. It was very convincing indeed.

The best of a scant number of political films was, at that, one of the best of all the films of 1976, *All the President's Men*, again directed by Pakula with an uncommon ability to convey the tension or the menace in seemingly ordinary situations. With Dustin Hoffman and Robert Redford as the principal exposers of the Watergate scandal, Carl Bernstein and Bob Woodward, the film defied the wisdom about politics as bad box office. It dramatized an ongoing national suspense story and it was by its nature a crackling good detective-spy story, mysterious informants and all.

The fears of the corrupting power, moral or political, of the movies would be alarming if justified; there is, however, a lack of solid and persuasive evidence either to convict or acquit the movies of having baleful effects on us. We know they can touch us. We cringe before their violence or are reassured and uplifted by their romantic idealism. What is less clear is whether, or how much, the movies *change* us. Do they make us, or only mirror us? Do they shape us as well as see us? In this day of the screen's new powers of expression, has it acquired new powers of persuasion or provocation as well? What are the movies saying to us? What are they *doing* to us?

The simple (and not overly helpful) answer surely is that there is a kind of continuous interaction between the movies and the society from which they arise. Very often what a movie says is less important than its existence. Nothing about *I Am Curious Yellow* (1967) or *Beyond the Valley of the Dolls* (1970) was as significant as the fact that they were able to be made and become notorious. Today, however, they would no longer cause much stir: they seem to have come from a world already remote.

Historical decadence, recorded in Satyricon, *proved to have much contemporary relevance as Federico Fellini saw it in his film.*

A modern scandal, Watergate, became a chilly suspenseful drama, with Robert Redford and Dustin Hoffman in All the President's Men.

It is inaccurate to claim that the movies are able to persuade us that we are different from the people we really are—specifically, that we are actually worse, more licentious, and more degraded. But it would seem arguable that the movies, mirroring something about the way we live, the kind of people we are, reinforce the truth of what they see and disseminate it more widely throughout the society. Contemporary movies may reflect this broadened truth, so that there is a reverberation at work. If the movies do not actually initiate change in the society, they at least confirm it and may accelerate it.

Yet even with their new candor, there is still a time lag between what we do and what the movies say we do. They are a delayed-action mirror, a not-so-instant replay. The movies, to take just one example, did not invent mate-swapping: they were in fact among the last to hear about it. If it had not already existed, *Bob and Carol and Ted and Alice* and Hollywood would never have had the nerve to invent it. As it was, the movie weighed the phenomenon and found it wanting. The couples prudently, if comically, called off the trade.

The time lag in the movies' reporting of where we are and what we are up to is narrowing, and at present the movies are more concerned with making us forget where we are and what trouble we are in. Yet in the area, always sensitive, of sexual manners and mores, the movies even until now have been decidedly remiss in keeping up with us.

There was one wretched comedy called *Prudence and the Pill* (1968), but no film I am aware of has dealt meaningfully with the impact of the pill on the lives of women, married or single. Illegal abortion has seldom been handled as poignantly as it was in *Alfie* several years ago. Legal abortion, either as controversy or as fact of life, has hardly been reflected on the screen, even in passing.

Only a masochist would be waiting breathlessly for a terrific film about either birth control or abortion, but the point is that both have everything to do with major changes in social attitudes and in life styles—with a decline in the strength of the forces fighting both on moral grounds—and yet the movies have acknowledged the changes only grazingly.

Films have certainly acknowledged that the marriage of true minds stumbles into a lot more impediments than it used to (see Chapter 8), yet even in the most devastating

A depraved future, drug-drenched and gleefully violent as depicted in Anthony Burgess' novel, A Clockwork Orange, *became a controversial Stanley Kubrick film, with Malcolm McDowell. Kubrick saw society's braintampering as more evil than violence. Burgess found more hope than Kubrick.*

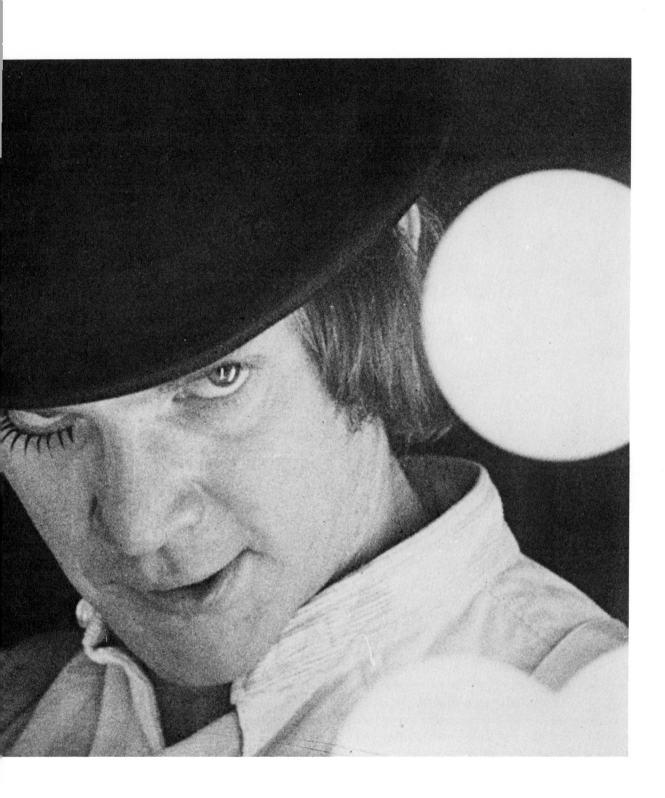

A *nuclear satire ending in holocaust, Kubrick's* Dr. Strangelove *(with Sterling Hayden and Peter Sellers) was hard on generals and politicians.*

portraits of marriage there is little suggestion of the *philosophical* trouble marriage is in. A younger generation—or at least many of its members—regards marriage as a possibility rather than a certainty, an alternative to be delayed or perhaps rejected entirely. It is still the most popular alternative, but the live-in relationship, conducted with all the fidelity of marriage but lacking the sanction of church or state, has become an unembarrassed and accepted life style. So far the movies have been able to make only embarrassed jokes about it. For all the commercial pressures on them to exploit and titillate, the movies remain (or end up) curiously chaste and traditional, less a floodgate to permissiveness than a bastion of orthodoxy.

It would be fascinating—if only it could be done—to measure the real influence the mov-

ies had on all of us who were growing up with them in the thirties, forties, and fifties, in the days of the Hays Code in all its rectitudinous glory. Our willing enslavement to the movies was total, and their moral vision was monolithic, a ceaseless reiteration of the verities, steadily presuming that we were in complete agreement as to what was good and desirable.

It would be no trouble to show that the movies influenced language, especially slang, and that they influenced fashions and fads heavily. They broke the tyranny of the black telephone by putting a white telephone in every boudoir, and made the rambling California ranch house a suburban must everywhere. It can be shown that the movies have influenced the way novelists write and what they say: Alfred Appel's *Nabokov's Dark Cinema* is an excellent study of Nabokov's massive borrowings from films, and when Prewitt in James Jones's *From Here to Eternity* talks about a sympathy for the underdog he got from movies of the thirties, one suspects that Jones did as well.

Prewitt's comments acknowledge the less obvious influences of the movies—all those assumptions, acquired in the dark, about how life was. How good prevailed in the end, and nice girls were virgins, and ministers were kind and wise, and things would get better than they were, sooner or later. Actually the assumptions were perhaps even more amorphous than that, a vague but solid hunch that the truth could be found and the answer was clear, and that *something would happen in time.* Better to trust with a brave heart and run the risk of being tricked by the unscrupulous than to sneer cynically and miss the chance, because those who trusted and dared would be rewarded in the end and the tricksters done in. But the cynics outsmarted themselves every time. Optimism was all, and the movies in the thirties were not wrong to stress it: there were plenty of reasons for pessimism in the world beyond the foyer.

And the movies always reflect the times in which they arise. How could it be otherwise, since they are the work of men and women who live in the society and in the times? Optimism was a major tenet of the American faith, and it still is, battered though it may be. The movies professed that the pursuit of happiness led to the simple life, but their vision of the good life was always rich in material comforts. (Half the films of the thirties seemed to be set in penthouses.) Maybe it was only those of us who were young at that time who had the hard relearning to do, the contradictions to sort out between idealized

movie and real life with all its ambiguities and untidy problems. The world was not black and white but piebald, and I am not sure it was just the innocence of youth that was a casualty. It was an age of social innocence that was under terminal pressure from events, and the movies were watching, if only out of the corner of their eye.

The death of the Hays Code was the end of a creed, to which thirty years of filmmakers had sworn their allegiance, however reluctantly. Today the creed has been replaced by a much shorter article of faith: the responsibility and good taste of the artist. The consequence is that it is no longer possible to generalize about what "the movies" are saying any more than it is to make dogmatic statements about what "the novel" or "the theater" is saying. It is easier to know what the movies are *not,* and they are definitely no longer a collective act of moral advocacy or affirmation. They reflect as never before the multiplicity of life, diversity of every kind, including moral diversity. We are seen to be multiracial and multifaithed, traditionalist and anarchic, existential and predestinarian, optimistic and pessimistic, divided (even as individuals), between cynicism and idealism.

But even the diversity is not quite so simple and straightforward as it sounds. From the forced and unlikely optimism that prevailed for years, the movies have now swung in the opposite direction, exulting in their ability to show the negative side of life, brutish, cynical, despairing. A whole cycle of pictures showed us at our worst: dropped-out children lost in the gauzy fantasies of the drug culture, weakness and corruption among their parents, resentful hard-hat bigotry in the working class. They all came together horrifically in John Avildsen's *Joe* (1969), a low-budget film made memorable by sensitive direction and Peter Boyle's fine playing of the title role. Some of the same themes were explored in Milos

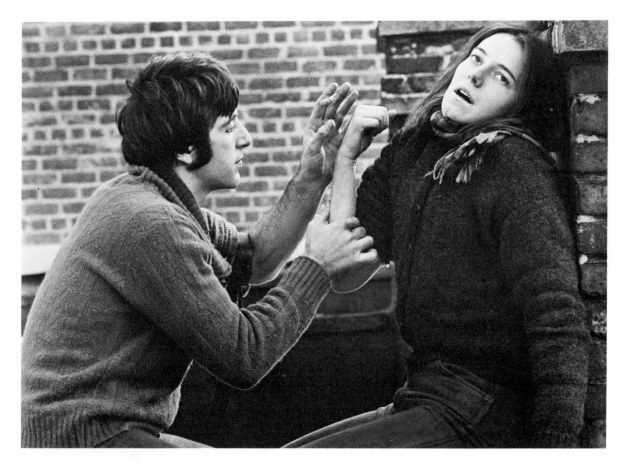

Forman's *Taking Off* (1971), but in a frame-work of black comedy.

The drug culture lent itself well to the trendy pessimism, and *The Magic Garden of Stanley Sweetheart, Cisco Pike, Dusty and Sweets McGee, Born to Win,* and *Panic in Needle Park*—all from the early seventies—shared an aura of hopelessness, although otherwise they were notably individual films.

The rise of the counterculture, like the women's movement a few years later, has been presented in the movies in the same sense that a rearview mirror catches a sunset: a glimpse rather than a reflection. *Easy Rider,* its open-air jauntiness growing darker with every mile, is probably still the best testimony the movies have given about the rupture in American life in the sixties. The rejection of traditional val-

Romeo and Juliet on junk, as it has been called, Panic in Needle Park *had Al Pacino and Kitty Wynn as young addicts, was too grim for audiences.*

ues, the quest for freedom within alternative life styles, the hatreds that crackled across the chasms not only of generation but of geography and attitude were all made personal in the Peter Fonda–Dennis Hopper film. It could be seen as a protest against everything that was repressive and lethal in the society, and yet its traveling characters also seemed to be discovering that they could not permanently escape all responsibility. Indeed, *Easy Rider* is not least a lament for the destruction of the family: the visit to a ranch family is pathetically wistful, as is a visit to a struggling commune, a new kind of family.

Much easier to take, Love Story *simply ignored reality and let Ali McGraw die beautifully as Ryan O'Neal watched bravely. It was a huge hit.*

Arthur Penn's *Alice's Restaurant* (1969) was a more subdued but more coherent look at the counterculture seen as an attempt to achieve a new kind of personal freedom within a new-style family, with Alice as the matriarch of a communal group living in a desanctified church. Penn melded fact and fiction, with the facts predominating, and imbued the film with a sense of his great personal concern for Alice and her brood. (Penn's home is not far from the actual restaurant in Stockbridge, Massachusetts.)

Both *Easy Rider* and *Alice's Restaurant* did well with audiences, in part, I think, because the melodramatics (in *Easy Rider*) and Arlo Guthrie's lopey comedy (in *Alice's Restaurant*) were tempered by tenderness and by the viewer's perception that both films were per-

sonal statements. Harder-edged and more calculated films did not prosper. Even if their pessimism could have been taken at face value and not seen as perversely chic (*Panic in Needle Park* was anything but chic), the unrelieved gloom was hard to take. The almost indecent popularity of *Love Story* in 1971 was a revelation and a turning, a multimillion-dollar reminder that audiences were athirst for romance and sweet suffering. The movie was more skillfully done than its harshest critics said it was, but above all it was lucky. It enjoyed the most fortuitous timing in recent movie history, arriving providentially as an an-

tidote to all the bad trips, cold turkeys, and dead ends.

The most conspicuous and interesting phenomenon of the movies in the early seventies was the appearance of black films. They were a godsend to Hollywood, revealing a rich market the studios had not so much overlooked as disdained, on the assumption that the black audience came along with the white audience and did not need special handling. In particular, the success of *Cotton Comes to Harlem* (1971), most especially in black neighborhoods where it sometimes outdrew *The French Connection*, opened industry eyes. Produced by Samuel Goldwyn Jr., *Cotton* had not been designed as a special-audience film, but the pattern of its popularity was carefully noted.

If there were any doubts about the existence of a viable black film audience, later the same year *Shaft* removed them. It was a huge success with both black and white audiences, as were most of the later blacksploitation films, as they came to be called. The formula was familiar: fast and violent private-eye action, sultry ladies, terse dialogue, vivid minor characters, a hero operating within the law, but just barely. If the formula was familiar, the face was not. But as the cool, tough Shaft in the original and two sequels, Richard Roundtree became a major black star, helping to break Sidney Poitier's lonely monopoly. There was irony in the fact that *The Learning Tree*, Gordon Parks's sensitive and well-done autobiographical feature film about his boyhood years in Kansas, had been a disappointment at the box office, while the more conventional *Shaft*, Parks's second film, became a blockbuster.

The new black films have been heavily criticized both within the black community and outside it for distorting the black experience as a whole, pandering to the lowest taste of any audience, and glorifying drug pushers (as

The parade of black films followed the success of Cotton Comes to Harlem, *which featured Calvin Lockhart as a con-man preacher.*

221

in *Superfly*) and other criminal types. It has also been argued that the black films are one more cynical rip-off of the blacks by the whites. There is truth in all the charges, but it is also true that the ugly white stereotypes in some of the black films are as unpleasantly racist as the shuffling, deferential Uncle Toms in yesterday's Hollywood film.

On balance, however, the net influence of the black films (which as an exploitation genre have peaked and begun to wane) will have been positive. An industry that had historically never used blacks behind the camera and had used them as performers only in limited and demeaning roles was almost overnight opened up to them. A large new genera-

tion of black performers has come to prominence: Roundtree, Jim Brown, Ruby Dee, Fred Williamson, Raymond St. Jacques, Diahann Carroll, Billy Dee Williams, William Marshall, Diana Ross, D'urville Martin, Roscoe Lee Browne, among innumerable others. There is also now a significant generation of black producers, directors, writers, as well as technicians.

The popularity of the black films parallels (and is symbolic of) a rising black consciousness and assertiveness. The heroics may be just as unbelievable as they are in the James Bond films and the contents are sometimes heavy-handed indeed, but characterization and milieu ring true. Much of the appeal of the black films has been, I think, in the shock of recognition they produce in their black audience. They reflect the realities of life in the urban ghettos with an unsparing accuracy, which previous movies had never (or almost never) done. Watching some of the films was a very uncomfortable experience for white audiences, exposing them to latent resentments and mistrust of the Man, making them feel for once the sting of stereotyping and ridicule. On the evidence of the protests, they also made uncomfortable viewing for many black middle-class professionals, who were furious that the films were as degrading to blacks as the "yassuh" servants used to be.

Again, an arguable point, but the indications already are that the kind of overstatement in the films was both inevitable and temporary, a phase. Just as television can be seen to have recapitulated the main strains of movie history into a quarter of a century, so the black films sometimes appear to have rolled eighty years of movie experience into half a decade. In not much longer than that, the black films have generated stars and creators, built up a new substructure for exhibition and distribution, and run through several genres-within-the-genre, most recently the black western, a cycle begun by *Buck and the Preacher* (1972) and followed by *Nigger Charlie* and several more low-budget, high-return quickies.

It was not clear, either to a skeptical Hollywood or to the black filmmakers themselves, whether a market existed for high-quality films about the black experience or only for the exploitive stuff. There were encouraging answers in the acceptance of Robert Radnitz's *Sounder* (1973), about a family of black sharecroppers in the Depression thirties, and fur-

A different black experience, the share-cropper's life, was dramatized in Robert Radnitz' Sounder, with Paul Winfield as a jailed father reunited with his son (Kevin Hooks).

ther encouragement in the even broader success of *Claudine* (1974), the tough but upbeat social comedy co-starring Diahann Carroll and James Earl Jones, and *Uptown Saturday Night* (1974), an all-star, easy-going comedy romp. All three films cut across racial lines in their popularity.

There will no doubt continue to be a market for the black exploitation movies, constituting at their least imaginative a kind of ghetto cinema. Yet one positive consequence

On the avenue, 5th Avenue, Michael Moriarty as a New York detective chases Tony King toward a Saks shoot-out in Report to the Commissioner.

of the phenomenon is that mainstream films that are not principally about race or aimed at a particular audience seem able to deal much less self-consciously with the racial diversity of the society. It begins to be both possible and likely that the movies will incorporate black life into a fairer representation of the national life than was possible in the past.

The Mike Frankovich production of *Report to the Commissioner*, released early in 1975, failed to find audiences, partly, I suspect, because of the extreme bleakness of its material. But it gave us a stunning portrayal by Yaphet Kotto as a black detective caught between black and white worlds, both of which distrust and reject him. The accuracy was brutal, but the honesty was welcome; Kotto emerged as the movie's most respected and sympathetic figure. A further problem

with the film was that the credibility of the Kotto character jarred against the cops-and-robbers melodramatics, including a rooftop chase through mid-Manhattan and a shootout in a Saks Fifth Avenue elevator.

It is indeed an uncertain time for any filmmaker, because the movies as mirror can give the world back to us with crystal clarity, free of all distorting ripples. But a little reality may not go far enough. Audiences are finding it harder to play the make-believe game. Swamped as we are by reality as reported by press, radio, and especially television, we are hard put to suspend disbelief even when we want to. The moonlit idyll in Central Park won't work, because we suspect there are muggers lurking behind every tree and bush even if the filmmaker has put none there.

Still, the concept of movies beginning with the reality of our times (even if the intent is to spin off dreams from the realities) is a good one. A pertinent rebuttal to the cry that movies and television may corrupt us is that they say so many different, often contradictory, things these days that they do not have the cumulative impact they once did. In their time of moral advocacy they may have appealed to and reinforced the best in us. Today their advocacy is as various as life itself, persuasive from moment to moment (we cannot doubt that there are men like the Yaphet Kotto detective, caught between worlds) but in effect they are offering evidence rather than conclusions.

I believe that just as governments exist by the consent of the governed, so movies exist (or succeed) by the endorsement of the marketplace, the public, and that the movies cannot stray too far from some sort of consensus. They can neither persuade us that we are radically different from the way we know ourselves to be nor convince us that we are more evil than we are. The movies may no longer hew to the specific moral criteria of the Judeo-Christian tradition, but they must still ultimately sit square with our transcendent awareness of human nature. That is, the movies cannot make any wide denial of our deepest ethical awarenesses, our sense that there is a knowable right and an identifiable wrong.

If we now speak of situational ethics, of understanding and doing what is right in a given circumstance, and if there is somehow understod to be an Eleventh Commandment that says, "Thou shalt not hurt another person," the movies will only at their peril fail to mirror those truths about the way we live. Even in fairly lighthearted moments, the movies now confront us with the ambiguities of the world, the knowledge that we are in-

Fascism was the politics of decadence in Visconti's The Damned, *with Dirk Bogarde and Ingrid Thulin as lovers and Nazis in pre-war Germany.*

fluenced by things said but not meant and meant but not said, the idea that things may not be as they seem. Contemporary films confirm our suspicion that the vision presented to us in earlier years—of a secure and settled order—was both limited and misleading because it obscured so many hard realities.

And yet in their openness, the movies are better equipped now than ever to remind us of our common humanity by helping us to see others as we see ourselves. The filmmaker, as Ingmar Bergman proves again and again, can probe our souls just as the novelist—or the theologian—does; and if he finds evil there, he finds faith and courage as well, and lends us hope against the shared night.

The uses of the past

Nostalgia, wrote Peter de Vries, isn't what it used to be. Except that for the movies it still is. The mastery over both space and time is at the heart of the magic of the movies. They were made for storytelling and they have always preferred "Once upon a time" to "This is how it is." Within the last dozen years the infatuation with the past has become obsessive, and there is no sign that the romance is cooling.

The uses of the past are various. Most often the movies (like the novel and the play) use the past as a refuge from a troubling present, returning to a time when life and living were simple and clear-cut (or, if they weren't, seemed so). The more difficult things get in the world outside the front door, the stronger the lure of other times becomes. Nostalgia may be a pleasure, but it is also a symptom, and the movies can't help revealing the national temperature. Presently there are more chills than fevers, with remedies sought in the days gone by.

The past is more than a hideaway, to be sure. Somewhere within it may lie clues as to who we are, where we are, and how we got here. Now as always there are movies digging for those clues, for guidelines that might make the present easier to comprehend. Then again, the filmmakers—the French, most particularly—have lately been looking at history more critically, examining some wartime events that ought not to be forgotten.

Hardly a decade has been left untouched by the film excursions to the past.

The sixties were affectingly memorialized in George Lucas's *American Graffiti* (1973), which withheld until the final cold reminder that the fun and games of some typical high school kids were a last romp before domesticity and death took over.

The fifties had their acrid nights in Bob Fosse's *Lenny* (1974), about a needling and needle-scarred comic who was perhaps a martyr but was also a pivotal figure in a time when we were turning from old puritanism to a new

An age of youthful innocence, high school in the California 1960s was remembered with style and affection in American Graffiti.

226

permissiveness. The final irony of Lenny Bruce was that a mainstream movie could be made of the material he was persecuted for using.

The forties had their most profitable day in *Summer of '42* (1973), Herman Raucher's sloshy and fantasized memory of coming of age on Cape Cod at the intersection of Booth Tarkington and Harold Robbins. It brought to mind George S. Kaufman's comment that what makes the good old days good is a bad memory. However romanticized its approach, the film touched an aging chord, and both the movie and its sequel, *Class of '44*, were successful.

The French, whose early forties were cruelly different from ours, have re-examined the period with a feeling that is anything but nostalgic, commencing with Marcel Ophuls's four-hour documentary about the Nazi occupation and the Vichy puppet government, *The Sorrow and the Pity* (1972). Michel Drach's *Les Violons du Bal (Violins at the Ball)* and Michel Mitrani's *Les Guichets du Louvre (The Gates of the Louvre)*, both in 1974, dramatized the November day when the Germans and their French collaborators rounded up all the Jews of Paris and herded them off to the camps, from which fewer than fifty ever returned.

Drach's film contrasts the secure and settled prewar life with the terrors of a family attempting to escape to Spain, based on his own boyhood experience. Mitrani's *The Gates of the Louvre*, adapted from a novel, focuses on the single day of the mass arrests and on a student who wants to help someone —anyone—escape the dragnet. Swift vignettes reveal the trusting passivity of many of the Jews, unwilling to believe their fellow Frenchmen would send them to their deaths, and reveal as well the smirking satisfaction of the anti-Semites and the helpless horror of those who could only watch as the vans were loaded and driven off.

Fleeing the Nazis in Les Violons du Bal, *mother and son (Marie-Josée Nat and David Drach) crouch at a fence near the border.*

228

In *Lacombe, Lucien* (1974), Louis Malle explores the personality of a Nazi collaborator, a brutish peasant boy inadvertently drawn into service with the Gestapo in a provincial village. From a small canvas Malle makes a large indictment, coolly drawn, of the spoiled aristocrats, cashiered policeman, riff-raff, and black marketeers who for a moment had their revenge on a society that had had no use for them. Even more important, Malle's film is a sermon on chance, the inadvertences of history that make a villain of Lacombe as casually as they could have made him the Resistance hero he first wanted to be.

The real events of the Nazi era produced one of the major films of 1976, *Voyage of*

A Gestapo recruit (Pierre Blaise) taunts a Jewish tailor (Holger Lowenadler) in Louis Malle's study of betrayal, Lacombe, Lucien.

the Damned, directed by Stuart Rosenberg from a script by Steve Shagan and David Butler, about a shipload of Jews, a few just out of concentration camps, sailing from Hamburg in May 1939, to Havana, to begin a new life in exile. But the Cubans had never intended the refugees should disembark; the United States refused to allow the ship to land and her captain reluctantly headed back toward Hamburg while diplomats negotiated an alternate harbor. What was remarkable in the context of the 1970s was that Britain's Sir

Lew Grade wagered nearly $9,000,000 on a grueling and shameful episode—although also a suspenseful and finally a heroic one—out of an unlamented past. An international ensemble of star actors led by Max von Sydow, Oskar Werner, and Faye Dunaway re-created the events with skill and dignity, and the story was a prickling reminder that man's capacity for inhumanity to man did not end with the voyage.

If the past wears many guises in film, the thirties—the most popular of the decades—shows most of them.

The Sting (1973), which has doubtless done more than any other movie to ensure that nostalgia will not die, used the thirties as the majority of the nostalgist movies do, as a place safely removed from ordinary reality. Robert Redford and Paul Newman, in their Arrow shirts, operated in a make-believe milieu that looked like the thirties but that in its pleasing storybook simplicity could be a kind of Graustark for grifters.

Bonnie and Clyde (1967) worked as a popular and essentially romantic entertainment, a jaunty comedy gradually building toward not-quite-tragedy and superviolent death. Yet

The past as a refuge from reality worked elegantly in Murder on the Orient Express, *Albert Finney as Detective Hercule Poirot examining a very starry cast of Agatha Christie suspects.*

it used the past as more than a mere refuge. The Benton-Newman script (with adjustments by Arthur Penn and, uncredited, by the Robert Towne who returned to the period in *Chinatown*) contemplated the past to explain the making of folk heroes of Clyde Barrow and Bonnie Parker as fighters against a banking system at once oppressive and failing.

One of Robert Altman's best movies, *Thieves Like Us* (1973), looked at a less glamorous criminal thirties. It depicted a Bonnie-and-Clyde kind of a gang who had none of the mythic claims of Bonnie and Clyde; they wound down to a bad end with no overtones of glory.

The Roman Polanski–Robert Towne *Chinatown* (1974) was another unapologetic entertainment that in part celebrated an entertainment form—the private-eye novel and film—but that also, and not incidentally, looked at the workings of power and greed and their part in the making and shaping of Los Angeles. And if the lustrous and detailed evocation of Los Angeles in the thirties said "once upon a time," the echoes of the film suggested that greed and corruption were neither dead nor confined solely to Los Angeles.

Murder on the Orient Express (1974) is so purely escapist that it fits any period and is hard to place in real time. But its triggering event was clearly taken by Agatha Christie from the Lindbergh kidnapping of the early thirties, which was probably also the peak period of the intricately plotted and splendidly artificial murder mystery. The nostalgia aroused by Sidney Lumet's glowing, ingenious diversion is accordingly for the dying elegance of the aristocratic purlieus of the prewar thirties.

The movies have fairly often made movies about the movies, if they have not often made them well. But until recently the movies have been oddly shy about acknowledging the influence they have had on our lives. The cam-

Fellini's look homeward to his boyhood, Amarcord, *featured a mock wedding of Fascist youth beneath a floral portrait of* Il Duce *himself.*

era may move self-consciously by a marquee displaying the title of another of the studio's films, but the movies have been the last to tell how they have suffused our days and nights. The French have been better about it, and half the films of the New Wave seem, one way or another, to have paid homage to other movies, mostly American. Truffaut's *Day for Night* (1974) is a sort of ultimate testament to the fascination of films from childhood on, for all of us.

Federico Fellini's *Amarcord* (1974), his reminiscence of growing up in provincial Rimini, makes the cinema the center of the town's nightlife, as it was, and the source of its images. The theater manager dresses in conscious imitation of Ronald Colman, and that's what the townspeople have nicknamed him. The town's principal prostitute dreams of finding her own Gary Cooper and getting out of the game, which at last she does. Laurel and Hardy are promised for next week, as they were in towns far removed from Rimini.

Increasingly now there are films offering a kind of double-decker nostalgia, not only presenting the past for its own sake but centering on the movies themselves as part of that past. *That's Entertainment* (1974) has been an overwhelming success with its well-assembled sampling of studio craftsmanship at its flamboyant best, the stars in their days of glory, and escapist romanticism at its purest. No wonder it has a sequel, *That's Entertainment Part Two* (1976). There is little doubt that the raidings of the Hollywood vaults will go on and on.

Mel Brooks's *Young Frankenstein* (1974) was a meticulously detailed homage to the original sound version of *Frankenstein* and to the look and feel of the horror films of the thirties. The pleasure of Brooks's comedy was that in all its updated craziness it retained an evident, felt affection for the tradition. Without that sense of homage the movie might have been much less affecting.

Most of Peter Bogdanovich's films to date have been tributes to the kinds of movies he grew up loving, and studying. The best of them was his first major feature, *The Last Picture Show* (1971), an elegiac tribute to the small-town movie house as a passing landmark, symbolic as well of the decline of small towns throughout the United States. Even more subtly, the movie seemed to pay tribute, perhaps unconsciously, to the way the movies reported on small-town life. The characters in *The Last Picture Show*, although made notably individual by the excellent performers,

Paying homage to the movie past, Mel Brooks used the original lab for his Young Frankenstein, *with Gene Wilder as the experimenter and Peter Boyle as his tall but kindly creation.*

could also be seen as types—the neglected wife, the sweet moron, the philosopher, the failed, the hopeful—who, although certainly present in real life, had been stereotyped in films.

In *What's Up Doc?* (1972) Bogdanovich tried less successfully (except at the box office: it was a hit) to catch the fast, madcap, wacky romanticism of the Howard Hawks comedies of the thirties. If he failed it was partly because they no longer make stars in the same larger-than-life dimensions as Cary Grant and Irene Dunne, among many others.

Hollywood itself—the process, not the product—has lately come in for revisionist scrutiny, nostalgist in the sense that anything dealing with the past is nostalgist, yet not entirely warming. By the time *The Way We Were* (1973) was released, it had lost most of its references to the hateful decade or more when the film industry was being ripped apart over charges of communist infiltration (Chapter 13). Arthur Laurents's original story was about a successful writer who leaves his political-activist wife to save himself from blacklisting. Only traces of the background, the protests, the hearings, and the firings remain, and they are fairly confusing. The decision was probably justified commercially: as a straight romance *The Way We Were* was a box-office bonanza.

John Schlesinger's *Day of the Locust* (1975), from the bitter novel by screenwriter Nathanael West, manages a gorgeously detailed re-creation of the studio Hollywood and the stucco and seedy residential Hollywood of the 1930s. But, although both the novel's and the movie's central figures are an ambitious young artist out of Yale eager to design movies and a dim-witted blonde with dreams of becoming another Jean Harlow, *The Day of the Locust* is primarily about a symbolic Hollywood that is the focus of all the gaudy, false, doomed dreams of a system that West pessimistically saw as a trap for all who lived and worked within it. The movie, even more than the book, confirms the apocalyptic uneasiness of the late thirties and makes the insane riot at the end seem an actual rather than a surrealist nightmare. Although the movie is less successful than it might have been, too consciously and coolly artful and detached, it is still an effective capturing of the dream factory at its most powerful—the maker of dreams but the focus of dreams, too.

Probably the best of the novels about the Hollywood of the late 1930s, F. Scott Fitzgerald's unfinished *The Last Tycoon*, with its insightful portrait of a creative studio boss much like Irving Thalberg, was disappointingly and clumsily adapted to the screen in 1976 by producer Sam Spiegel, director Elia Kazan, and writer Harold Pinter. Robert DeNiro's spiritual and physical resemblance to Thalberg was uncanny, and in its fleeting best moments the movie showed the head of production furiously at work, changing directors in mid-film, coddling and consoling stars, setting writers straight, barking orders after watching the daily rushes, contending with the money moguls who distrusted and hated his arrogant confidence. But too often the story surrendered to an ill-cast, inappropriately written and very tiresome romance, and the result was neither an illumination nor an affectionate recreation of the Golden Age.

What the movies have seldom done, so far, is to see nostalgia as nostalgia, to examine the wistful longing for the past. Yet two movies have tried to do it and have managed surprisingly well. The nostalgia of the Jack Lemmon character in *Save the Tiger* (1973) is focused on baseball and big bands rather than movies (although a strange and ironic secret meeting takes place in the balcony of a downtown Los Angeles movie temple now showing porno films). And the character's feeling that values were clearer and life simpler and more hope-

Hollywood hopefuls in Day of the Locust, *adapted from Nathanael West's bitter novel, Karen Black and William Atherton were going noplace.*

ful (if not easier) in the days of Bunny Berrigan and Cookie Lavagetto is made unbearably poignant against the detailing of his present how-did-it-happen corruption.

In *Summer Wishes, Winter Dreams* (1973), Joanne Woodward's girlhood lives on in fantasy as a place to which she hopes to return—an unworkable fantasy, as her unsympathetic and tough-minded daughter points out. The collapse of the fantasy and the temporary collapse of her personality are the core of the movie. Martin Balsam as her husband finds in his own battlefield memories at Bastogne a renewed sense of his own worth, if also a reminder that the world and time move on. The past, understood and left in place, arms the couple in Stewart Stern's story to pick up their ongoing lives with tranquility, if without dreams.

The movies can go home again, but they can't really live there any more than the rest of us can. Although escapist visits to the past have charm and poignance, there is a risk in imagining that the past is the only vein the movies have to mine. The simplicity of life as the movies of the thirties saw it is wistfully attractive, which is why the movies of the thirties are so newly popular. But things aren't what they used to be. No, and they never were.

237

Hollywood and the future

Late in 1965—not much more than a decade ago—when I first surveyed Hollywood for the *Los Angeles Times,* Jack L. Warner was running the studio that bore his name, and Walt Disney was running his. Mike Frankovich was in charge of production at Columbia, Robert Weitman at MGM, Howard W. Koch at Paramount, Richard Zanuck at Fox (while his father tried to fight off the stock raiders in New York). Bob Blumofe was the West Coast head of production for United Artists and Edward Muhl was handling the film side of Universal under president Lew Wasserman.

All, all are gone.

Jack Warner sold his interests, and his studio has changed owners twice. Walt Disney and his brother Roy are both dead, but the company prospers mightily under Cardon E. Walker, with something like half the business volume coming from Disneyland and Disney World rather than the movies. Frankovich, Weitman, Koch, Zanuck, and Blumofe are all successful independent producers. Columbia,

after stock control fights, executive shakeups, and some catastrophically bad years, has made a comeback under new leadership and with the help, timely but now eliminated by Congress, of tax shelter money. Metro came under the control of Kirk Kerkorian, a financier who cut production back to almost nothing and liquidated many of the company's assets to build the Grand Hotel in Las Vegas, which (confounding Kerkorian's critics) has turned out to be enormously profitable. Paramount has since become part of Charles Bluhdorn's conglomerate, Gulf & Western, and has had several shifts in creative leadership. New majority owners at Fox ousted the Zanucks and a new corporate leader, Dennis Stanfill, oversees what is now a second wave of production bosses. United Artists, now a subsidiary of Transamerica, a San Francisco–based conglomerate, has changed production heads, although its top management in New York remains the same. Lew Wasserman is still the head man at Universal, although he presides

A perfect clown for a new day, Woody Allen is his own writer, producer, director, and also star—creating a character who is a kind of post-graduate Everyman, neurotic but nice.

Cold as the Devil can make him, Jason Miller as
The Exorcist *fights for the life and soul of a young*
girl in the supernatural film hit.

over a much-revised creative management team, with Sidney Sheinberg his second in command.

Motion picture hierarchies have always been volatile, but this unprecedented impermanence in the executive suites perfectly symbolizes the fundamental changes in Hollywood, from the age of the moguls to the age of the professional managers, who tend in fact to have been agents, lawyers, comptrollers. The moguls are gone and so are the concentrations of power they controlled. Movies are still a potent and popular enterprise, but the industry that makes, sells, and shows them—always loose and competitive within itself—has in the age of television divided into more and smaller concentrations of power. There are more distribution firms, more independent production firms, more theater chains. The majors, except for Universal, aren't as major as they used to be. MGM, whose distribution organization was worldwide, now has none at all and releases its few films through United Artists.

Hollywood's theatrical film output continues to decline, and in late 1976 the shortage of popular new movies was so acute that many first-run cinemas were showing revivals of *Woodstock,* the films of Stanley Kubrick, classic packages from Warner's and MGM. In New York, several first-run theaters closed down, at least temporarily, because they could find nothing to show that anyone wanted to see.

The great days of the movies are gone, and they aren't coming back. The steady audience is gone. A survey conducted for the Motion Picture Association in the late sixties reported that every other person in the United States never goes to the movies at all. But there is evidence that the worst days for the movies may be over, too. In 1975 the average weekly attendance (reflecting the phenomenal popu-

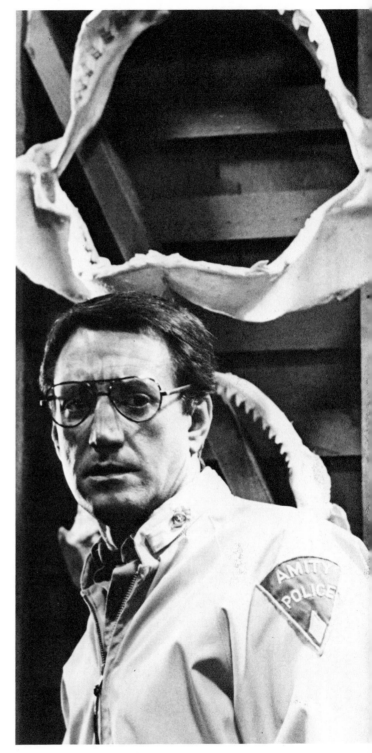

The largest-grossing film of all time, Jaws *has earned nearly $200 million for Universal, proving that audiences like a good scare. Roy Scheider was the police chief, gritting his teeth against panic.*

larity of *Jaws*) was back up to nearly 20 million, the highest since 1963, and the gross annual take at the box office was $2.1 billion, the highest ever, although that figure reflected the inroads of inflation.

Going out of the house and into the neutral, comfortable, common darkness of a theater, in the presence of others with whom one shares the experience, is part of the movie mystique, part of the dream-like state that watching a movie is. Going out is not the same as watching a movie at home, no matter how safe, comfortable, and convenient the living room may be, and no matter how large the television images become. The special nature of going out to the movies is probably their last line of resistance in the face of television's broadening freedom of expression, but it is a formidable last line of resistance.

The movie audience is unpredictable and vigorously selective, but it is still there and it is interested. The customers are willing to defy the elements, the price, the parking, and the unruly streets to see the movies they want to see: *The Exorcist, The Godfather, Jaws, One Flew Over the Cuckoo's Nest, Blazing Saddles, Benji,* or a work as grueling as Ingmar Bergman's *Face to Face*. This loyalty, and the breadth of choice over which it is exercised, have to be consoling and reassuring for all those who care about the health and vitality of the movies as an art form.

Everything that is true about the movies today and tomorrow is made true by the audience, and the same survey in the late sixties that brought the sad tidings that half of us never go to the movies at all had other tidings as well. The present audience is different in both size and makeup. It is younger and brighter. The shift toward a younger audience had, according to some small testings, begun in the 1930s, even before television. By now, the most recent samplings taken for the Motion Picture Association disclose that nearly 90 percent of all movie tickets are bought by

Rejected by the majors, Cuckoo's Nest *was finally financed by a record company, and became an Oscar-winning hit for Jack Nicholson and friends.*

242

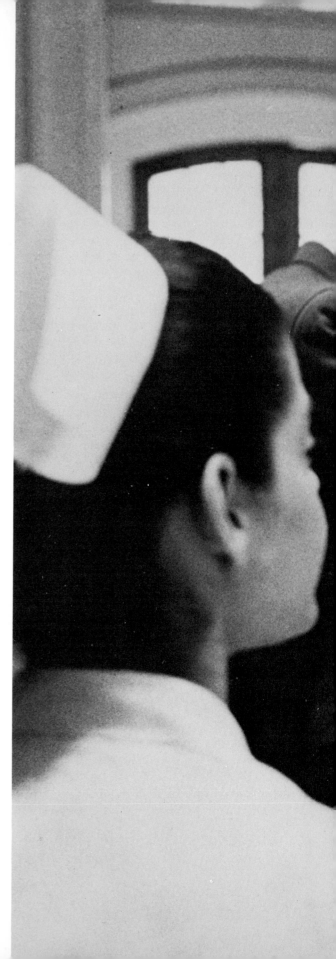

those between the ages of 12 and 39 (although they represent less than 60 percent of the total population). The McLuhan generation—and those who are now 40 were still in grade school when television began—really does dig the flicks.

There is also evidently a direct correlation between education and interest in the movies. The Daniel Yankelovich survey for the MPAA in the late sixties discovered that those who attend the movies least often are apt to be those who are beyond high school age but who did not finish high school. Roughly speaking, the more education, the more interest in the movies, which is a 180-degree turn from the early days when the movies belonged to the working class and were disdained as vulgar by the elite.

Television is naturally the principal author of the changes in the movie audience, and it is accordingly responsible for changes in the standards and expectations of that audience. John Culkin of the Center for Understanding Media once estimated that by the time a student has finished high school he or she has spent approximately 11,000 hours in the classroom, but more than 13,000 hours watching television, and has seen perhaps 600 movies, on television or in theaters. (Because some of the classroom hours were undoubtedly spent watching educational films, the exposure to the visual experience is even higher.)

This superindoctrination of images has had its effect. Handily summed up, it is that the present moviegoer may not know what he likes, but he knows what is bad, having watched so much of it. Audiences no less than critics know when a film has failed to live up to its expectations. When it fails, neither stars nor expensive promotion campaigns will save it. The critics may be appalled (though not often surprised) by some movies that find great favor with audiences, yet many of these films have something special going for them, if only novelty (such as the trained rats in

Shooting his way to success, Robert De Niro played the young Brando role in Godfather II, *which bracketed the events of the original film.*

Willard). If the original *Airport* was old-fashioned hokum, it was sleekly made hokum. The film may also have had a strong if subliminal appeal to those who take pride in their work and who had a chance to watch actors depicting characters (engineer George Kennedy, manager Burt Lancaster) who took pride in theirs.

The moguls in their day had it easy in many ways. They were playing to a mass audience whose members went to the movies regularly if they went at all. Today moviegoing as a habit survives mostly among the dating young. There are some indications that over-40s, among whom the most drastic falling away from the movies took place, have slowly begun to attend again, although unpredictably. But the moguls not only had a large and steady audience, they also had an audience with whose needs, tastes, and aspirations they were in close touch. There is a famous rude anecdote about the whole world being wired to Harry Cohn's restless rear end, but it was, in a sense, true. He and Jack Warner and Louis B. Mayer—and Walt Disney, who never forgot what it was to grow up poor—had no trouble understanding their customers' desires for escape, excitement, romance, and hope.

The newer (and for the most part more temporary) studio bosses have a harder time figuring out who and where the patrons are. There was once that lovely mass audience:

now there are audiences, worryingly capricious, for comedy, action, horror, romance, violence, family films, black films, foreign films, all-star spectacles, disasters. Outside the mainstream there is an audience for porno films, although there are signs that this audience is diminishing as the curiosity wears off.

It is the unpredictability of the audience that makes for the nervousness and the turnover in the executive offices. Although they had relatively little promotion in the beginning, for example, Tom Laughlin's *Billy Jack* (1971) and Bing Crosby Productions' *Walking Tall* (1973) both became maverick successes in Middle America, well before they found their metropolitan admirers. Both developed cultlike followings (and engendered sequels) for their violent excitements and their central figures, courageous loners battling corrupt establishments. What may be most noteworthy about those two hits is that, like the family film *Benji* (financed and distributed by a new Dallas firm) and even *Cuckoo's Nest*, they had their origins outside the major studios.

If there has been a trend in Hollywood moviemaking in the late 1970s, it has been toward safety and caution, for several reasons. Costs are a crucial item. Inflation has hit the major studios as hard as or harder than the rest of the economy. Few movies are being made and each costs more, which breeds caution. Caution in this sense means buying well-publicized novels or plays rather than originals and casting expensive stars rather than unknowns. In the further logic of the industry, caution means spending more in the hope of making more.

The fact that the new managers are not necessarily filmmakers (and in most cases don't claim to be) also breeds caution. Lacking the intuitive feeling for the form that their predecessors usually had and without any sure sense of where the audience is, they must rely on the feel of a package deal (prop-

A family film made outside the industry by a young Dallas firm, Benji *proved that dogs are cute and audiences can be found.*

erty, star or stars, director) presented by agents, hefting it against the conventional wisdom of the moment as to who or what is hot. The resurgence of the superstar system, the male branch anyway, has been triggered by the conventional wisdom (shored up by the grosses just often enough), and so has the persistence of violence, disaster, hide-my-eyes nostalgia, films that in any genre have a curiously impersonal glaze over their people and events.

The veteran director of *It Happened One Night* and *Mr. Smith Goes to Washington,*

The "sleeper" hit of 1976, Rocky, shot for only $1.3 million, was written by and also stars young Sylvester Stallone as an underdog who makes good.

Frank Capra, gazing around at the current movie scene not long ago, said, "People don't change, audiences don't change. They want romance and hope, heroes willing to fight for things they believe in. If I were making films today, I'd still make my kind of films. Update them, of course, but the essentials would be the same. The human heart doesn't change."

The tardy discovery of the late seventies could prove to be that Capra is right. The "sleeper" film of the 1976 Christmas season was *Rocky*, perhaps the most Capraesque film in years with its celebration of an uncommon common man. It was written by and stars a young Italian-American named Sylvester Stallone, whose central figure has echoes of Ernest Borgnine in *Marty* and Marlon Brando in *On the Waterfront*. Rocky, like the waterfront Brando, is a prizefighter who's never had a break. Unlike Brando, Rocky gets one. But the story is much less about boxing than about the possibility of hope when it is inspired by the love and support of a good woman (Talia Shire).

Rocky, like Hal Ashby's meticulously honest and deeply admiring biography of folk singer Woody Guthrie, *Bound for Glory*, also released at Christmas time, suggested that the humanist impulse that animated so many great movies through the years might be felt again in American productions. There were some glorious imported movies in 1976 that, in their concern for the fates of roundly portrayed individuals (and, of course, in their popularity with American audiences), seemed likely to lend encouragement to writers, producers, and executives eager to provide alternatives to car chases and lighter-than-air returns to a past that never was.

Cousin, Cousine was the foreign sleeper of the year, a romantic satire on French bourgeois family life but a film whose central love story was so attractively played that the satiric elements were half-forgotten by the time the enchanted viewers got home and the critics

An imported delight, Cousin, Cousine *is a grown-up love story from France starring Marie-Christine Barrault and Victor Lanoux.*

Tavernier's first feature was amazing in the unassertive economy with which it conveyed the flavor of the father's life, thought, work, neighborhood, and society, as well as the son's (with an oblique but telling glimpse of a factory and a sleazy boss). Tragedy reconciles father and son, and the joy of it (for them as well as for the audience) outweighs everything else.

A lesser but often very funny and affecting comedy, Yves Robert's *Salut L'Artiste* (*Hail, Artist*), examined a drastically different kind of life: Marcello Mastroianni's as a middlingly successful actor living and working in Paris. To keep afloat, he dashes from sub-Sellers slapstick movies to costume dramas, to a cabaret magic act, to a walk-on in a stage detective melodrama, all the while vacillating between a dishy ex-wife (Carla Gravina) he has to meet on the sly and the nifty person (Françoise Fabian) he currently lives with. Mastroianni, in one of the best roles he has had since he was Fellini's world-weary journalist in *La Dolce Vita*, creates a sadly comical figure, a nice guy adrift not in the jaded *dolce vita* world but in a world that is shifting, distracted, impermanent, elusive, permissive of almost everything save continuity and stability.

What all of these films—even the big budget and wide-ranging *Bound for Glory*—had in common was the quality of intimacy, of fetching the viewer close enough to detect the heartbeats of a character or two or three or four whom the viewer came to understand, recognize if not identify with, and care about.

The quality of intimacy is not readily created by studio committees, and it is rarely an ingredient in the kinds of star packages that are offered to the decision makers in the film world of the late 1970s. The intimate films are usually works of individual passion in the making—an individual intelligence like Tavernier nursing a first effort with loving care, or a small group so firmly in accord on their in-

reached their typewriters. Marie-Christine Barrault and Victor Lanoux played cousins by marriage, each stuck in an unhappy marriage and splendidly vulnerable to each other as they met at yet another of the winey family weddings. It was not at all clear that they would live happily ever after, but at least they had found happiness and had had the courage to seize it with a thumb of the *nez* at hypocritical conventions.

There were other French imports that upheld the humanist tradition of that country's best films. Bertrand Tavernier's *The Watchmaker of St. Paul's*, taken from a Georges Simenon novel, examined with subtlety and sympathy a man's relationship with his estranged son during a few weeks when the son, implicated in a murder, is a fugitive.

The director's director, the durable Orson Welles made Citizen Kane *at 25 and it still leads critics' polls as the best film of all time.*

*The master of suspense, Alfred Hitchcock made
his Family Plot at 77 and is vigorously planning
the next, after 55 years in film.*

A German genius, Fritz Lang specialized in emotional intensities; M is his masterpiece.

The great Italian director Vittorio De Sica's kind of realism changed the course of film history.

tentions as to be a single intelligence, and here the producers, the writer-star, and the director of *Rocky* come to mind.

One central casualty of the decline of the studios has been the staff producer who in his heyday was a general in command of all the elements of a movie, including the director, and who had (if he was any good, and survived) not only power but knowledge and his own passion for good work. He has latterly been replaced by the producer as money-finder, which is no mean skill but is not much help in the creative collaboration that makes movies. There are few so-called *auteur* producers in the tradition of Goldwyn, David O. Selznick, and the still-active Hal Wallis, whose own signatures were visible in their work. Robert Evans (*Chinatown, Marathon Man*) and the team of Richard Zanuck and David Brown (*Sugarland Express, Jaws*) are among the surprisingly few producers who presently appear to have strong affinities for the shaping as well as the financing of their movies.

The decline of the creative producer has hurt the cause of film both in the United States and abroad, because it has meant more movies with the plastic-wrapped blandness of committee decision and fewer with that unmistakable charge of personal commitment. This is, of course, the old tension between movie art and movie commerce expressed in another way. The pressures in the seventies that make for caution are pressures in favor of commerce at the sacrifice of art. The exasperating thing for the critic, as for any dedicated moviegoer, is that the cynical commercial wisdom so often falls on its face and the "risky" ventures (defined now as moderate cost films without major stars) succeed spectacularly. And the undertakings, large or small, that do come off well have that aura of personal care (true even of *Jaws*, which Zanuck and Brown personally saw through some logistical nightmares).

An aristocrat by birth, Luchino Visconti moved from themes of social protest to films, like his Death in Venice, in which decor mirrored souls.

The most successful woman director today, Italy's Lina Wertmuller began as an aide to Fellini, won international acclaim for her Love and Anarchy.

A wonderful diversity has always marked the movies. With production at less than half its historic levels, the movie buff's best hope for the future is that the diversity can somehow still be sustained.

The painful readjustment to the hard truths of the television age goes on for the movies. The old baroque movie palaces in the city centers are almost all dead and gone, replaced by smaller cinemas in suburban shopping centers and by multiple cinemas that have from two to six screens under one roof, all serviced by one box office, one projection room—and one candy counter. The multiplex cinemas, as they are called, accommodate the smaller size and wider tastes of present audiences, and their locations reflect the needs for parking and for some sense of personal security.

The smaller houses, more economical to operate, make it possible for specialized movies (documentaries, say, or "difficult" foreign films) to find their audiences and earn their way. Nevertheless, the high cost of opening and showing a movie is another of the cruel facts of film life today. Estimates are that it costs a minimum of $50,000 a week (in theater rental and advertising) to launch a commercial movie in New York or Los Angeles, and is comparably expensive in other metropolitan cities. Consequently, unless a movie shows early promise of being a hit, it is shelved very quickly to await the sale to television that will minimize the losses, anyway. As a matter of fact, if a movie does terribly in sneak previews, it may not even be released at all. A few years ago, Bob Thomas of Associated Press made a survey that revealed there were movies never publicly screened that had cost a total of $100 million sitting in the studio vaults.

Fewer movies than ever return their costs (one in 25 by one guess, although the bookkeeping in Hollywood is so byzantine that it is hard to say, and even harder to know what

255

anybody means by profits). But the returns on the successes are so whopping that the lure for entrepreneurs is irresistible. One new wrinkle in the seventies has been "four-walling," in which individuals or independent companies rent existing theaters for special engagements. Typically, the renters take over the theaters to the four walls, that is, renting on a flat fee basis and running the box office themselves. They take two dozen theaters or more in a major area, run a massive (and very expensive) blitz ad campaign on local television, and show their films for limited periods, usually two or three weeks. Unfortunately, the pictures themselves are usually poor stuff, cheaply assembled nature films, exploitation fare that seldom lives up to the provocative ads, foreign-made family fare that had very little to lose in translation.

The four-wall customers have been ripped off frequently enough to start approaching more cautiously, and there seems to have been a slow-down in the number of hard-selling four-wall operations. The device may prove to have merit in the long run as a way of releasing films that require special handling and that may not even be able to find a regular commercial distributor.

Writing in *Scribner's* magazine back in 1930, the early critic Pare Lorentz, who later made some classic documentaries (*The Plow That Broke the Plains, The River*), said, "The best technicians in the world are in Hollywood, and they have achieved beauty in form many times, but the content of their art remains childist. . . . It is no wonder that a trip to Hollywood is regarded by writers as a descent into hell, a free ride to a psychopathic ward, a fantastic dream of wealth without content. It is easy to understand why a socalled art that has risen to be a world industry monotonously produces vacuous, cheap, and banal entertainment."

There are still the vacuous, cheap, and banal entertainments, the formula films with

A patient perfectionist, David Lean, here filming a storm for Ryan's Daughter, *can make the epic intimate, as he did in* Lawrence of Arabia.

Gag writer turned comic turned director, nutty
Mel Brooks has made a string of hits from
The Producers *to the noisy* Silent Movie.

A film critic first, Peter Bogdanovich showed a flair for comedy in What's Up, Doc? *with Barbra.*

Cool intelligence and a way with suspense mark the work of Alan Pakula, whose best films include Klute *and* All the President's Men.

their mandatory unmotivated violence and their thin characters. Yet to read Lorentz's passionate lament of nearly a half-century ago is to realize what a long way, for all their flaws and their timidities, the movies have come. Out of their drastically altered financial condition and in the presence of their diminished audiences, the movies have achieved maturity, or the freedom of expression with which mature considerations of the world are possible.

There are motion pictures—even the updated *King Kong*—that would have astonished the young Lorentz and possibly dismayed Will Hays and Louis B. Mayer.

An art form has to be judged by its peaks as well as by its depths, and the best of the movies now being made give impressive witness to the diversity and complexity of life. The movies that evidently do best with audiences are those that speak to our resilient hopes and our traditional suspicion that good may win once in a while. The movies are better able to prove that we are flawed, fragile, capable of evil. But they cannot persuade us that we are debased, or that the world has changed in fundamental ways. In fact, the movies make our small triumphs, our inchings forward on the long march of civilization, our sheer dogged persistence all the more impressive and reassuring because they can be seen to have taken place in a recognizable reality.

Any forecast for the movies is bracketed with uncertainty, which is itself a form of optimism. The ruthless choosiness of the movie audience and the capricious fates of television conspire to make volatility the ongoing condition of the industry. The two forms keep shifting (sparring) in their relationship to each other. The demands of the audience change, and are marked by a quicker impatience. The prime function of movies and television, now as ever, is to entertain, but the meaning of entertainment seems to widen constantly, so

From Broadway as an actor-director, Mike Nichols did Virginia Woolf *as his demanding first film.*

From Poland, clearly with an eye for the macabre came Roman Polanski (Cul de Sac, Repulsion).

From England John Schlesinger (Billy Liar) *came to do the very American* Midnight Cowboy, Locust.

Fiercely independent, successful actor-director John Cassavetes depicts modern lives with raw power, as in his Woman Under the Influence.

much so that "to engross" might be a better term, because it would then embrace those experiences that are not, in a sense, strictly pleasurable.

It is worth noting that the most successful of television situation comedies, vintage 1976—"All in the Family," "The Bob Newhart Show," "The Mary Tyler Moore Show"—are often, though not always, dealing with real and unfunny human dilemmas (intolerance, the loneliness of the career girl, the ego-crushing aspect of unemployment). The problems are coated with humor, but they are also confronted rather than ignored or denied.

In one of his updated fairy tales, James Thurber gave us a new moral: little girls are harder to fool than they used to be. So are audiences: they are more aware of being manipulated, coddled, deceived, patronized. They are ready and willing to play make-believe, to be supplied with dreams, but it somehow has to be on terms that match their intelligence and their experience.

For all the pressures toward an evasive safety in the movies and a witless commercialism in television (as raucously decried in *Network*) in the short term, it is possible to be a long-term optimist for the future of both media. The selective perceptions of audiences will have their impact, and so will the new technologies and the new organizational structures of television and the movies.

Walt Whitman said that great poetry demands great audiences, and while *greatness* is an oversolemn and elusive word, there is no doubt that art and audiences are indissolubly linked. It is certain that changed audiences have evoked changed movies and altered our previous understanding of what was commercial. The newer flicks do not necessarily reject the fixed and kindly world of Andy Hardy: its wistful innocence touches us all. It is just that there is more to us, and there are other worlds, and the movies are getting around to them.

Readings

This book is not intended as a scholarly tome. I have spared you footnotes and other accessories. And the books represented by a "complete" bibliography of the best work now available on film history, filmmakers and films would spill off fifteen five-foot shelves, or fifty.

What follows is simply a kind of Desert Island Treasury of the film books I would not want to be without.

The basic one-volume reference work on the movies is still Leslie Halliwell's *The Filmgoer's Companion*, 4th ed. (New York: Hill & Wang, 1974), also available in paperback. Lively and opinionated, even in capsule form; illustrated, exhaustive, as seductive as peanuts or potato chips.

The basic one-volume history of the movies is still Arthur Knight's *The Liveliest Art* (New York: Macmillan, 1957), available in paperback. Knight is currently preparing a revised and updated edition, sure to be as urbane and informed as the first.

A larger, longer and more personal film history, particularly strong on current foreign language cinema everywhere on earth is *The Long View* by the British filmmaker Basil Wright (New York: Alfred A. Knopf, 1974).

The most eloquent testimony about the silent era, in words and pictures, is in Kevin Brownlow's *The Parade's Gone By*, in which the participants remember how it looked (New York: Alfred A. Knopf, 1969).

Bosley Crowther's companion volumes, *The Lion's Share: The Story of an Entertainment Empire* (New York: E.P. Dutton, 1957) about MGM and *Hollywood Rajah: The Life and Times of Louis B. Mayer* (New York: Holt, Rinehart & Winston, 1960) about the man who made MGM, both also illuminate the Hollywood of the Golden Age, and how it aged.

Jack Vizzard's account of the Breen office, *See No Evil: Life Inside a Hollywood Censor* (New York: Simon & Schuster, 1970) is an amusing and salty chronicle that stays relevant to the ratings problems in a later time.

Pre-television Hollywood times were described by Leo C. Rosten in *Hollywood: The Movie Colony, The Movie Makers* (New York: Harcourt, Brace, 1941).

A first-rate reference on the growth of electronic communications is *Broadcasting in America: A Survey of Television and Radio, 2d ed.* by Sydney W. Head (Boston: Houghton, Mifflin, 1972).

The neo-realist period, as well as everything that preceded and followed in Italian filmmaking is well-documented in Pierre Leprohon's work *The Italian Cinema* (New York: Praeger, 1972).

Two well-detailed books on women and movies are *From Reverence to Rape: The Treatment of Women in the Movies* by Molly Haskell (New York: Holt, Rinehart & Winston, 1973) and *Popcorn Venus; Women, Movies and the American Dream* by Marjorie Rosen (New York: Coward, McCann & Geoghegan, 1973).

The filmmakers themselves are probably best discovered in *The American Cinema* by this country's leading *auteur* theorist, Andrew Sarris (New York: E. P. Dutton, 1968). Sarris ranks and gives brief assessments of each of the major directors, sometimes raising hackles but providing an invaluable quick reference.

A recent and highly readable examination of the master director is *The Art of Alfred Hitchcock* by Donald Spoto (New York: Hopkinson and Blake, 1976).

The best criticism survives the test of time as judgment and as literature and becomes as well a source of film history. One of the country's finest critics was the late James Agee, whose *Agee on Film* (Boston: Beacon paperback, 1964) is indispensable, a guide to the films of the '40s and a sampling of reviews at their eloquent, penetrating compassionate best.

The collections of Pauline Kael are also lively reading. Her most recent volume is *Reeling* (Boston: Atlantic-Little, Brown, 1976).

The Hollywood past is illustrated in personal terms in a number of energetic memoirs. Perhaps the best and most unsparing is Frank Capra's *The Name Above the Title: An Autobiography* (New York: Macmillan, 1971). There are notably entertaining recollections from directors Raoul Walsh in *Each In His Own Time* (New York: Farrar, Straus and Giroux, 1974) and William Wellman in *A Short Time for Insanity* (New York: Hawthorne, 1974).

The range of decision-making that goes into any ambitious film is shown in remarkable detail in *Memo From David O. Selznick*, edited by Rudy Behlmer (New York: Viking, 1972), also available in paperback. Selznick's compulsive memo-making frazzled platoons of secretaries but left an unmatched account of the preparations for *Rebecca* and other films—including, of course, *Gone With the Wind*.

Mickey Rooney, whose own life was so unlike Andy Hardy's, has told it all in his breezy and refreshingly candid autobiography *I. E. An Autobiography* (New York: G. P. Putnam's Sons, 1965).

But, come to that, there is hardly a performer , a period a film genre, a filmmaker or a filmmaking that is not celebrated in one recent book or several. The movies may not be seen as often as they used to be, but they are regarded very seriously.

Credits

The author and the publisher would like to express their appreciation for use of the pictures in this book to the following.

A. B. Siensk Filmindustri: pp. 98–99
ABC (TV): pp. 196, 197, 198, 199, 204–205
ABC Pictures Corporation: p. 96
Academy Motion Picture Arts and Science: pp. 35, 42, 50–51, 61, 100, 115, 159
Avco-Embassy Pictures Corporation: pp. 78–79, 84–85, 113, 130
BIG BIRD © Muppets, Inc. 1971–77: p. 188.
CBS (TV): pp. 31, 190, 200–201, 206
Cinema Center Films: p. 147
Columbia Pictures Industries: pp. 22, 56–57, 58, 61, 80, 93, 102–103, 108, 111, 116, 122, 123, 134, 135, 151, 154–155, 176–177, 181, 183, 211, 216
Embassy Pictures Corporation: pp. 109, 260
Faces International Film Production: pp. 140, 261
KCET: pp. 192, 207, 252, 253
Libra Films: p. 250

Lucille Ball Productions: pp. 194–195
Metro-Goldwyn Mayer: pp. 3, 4, 5, 10, 20, 47, 71, 76, 83, 89, 117, 161, 163, 164, 167, 173, 222, 256–257
Midwest Film Productions: p. 143
Mulberry Square Productions: p. 247
NBC (TV): pp. 27, 28–29, 30, 32, 33, 187, 189, 191, 193
Paramount Pictures Corporation: pp. 44, 48–49, 82, 100, 126–127, 142, 148–149, 152–153, 160, 162, 174, 175, 209, 219, 231, 232–233, 237, 244–245, 260
Sheldrake Films, Ltd.: p. 180
20th Century-Fox: pp. 68–69, 72, 97, 101, 106–107, 128–129, 137, 141, 145, 150, 170–171, 218, 223, 230, 235
UCLA Theatre Arts Library: pp. 3, 4, 5, 6–7, 8, 9, 10, 13, 14–15, 16–17, 20, 36, 37, 38–39, 40–41, 47, 48–49, 63, 66–67, 71, 94–95, 105, 106–107, 110, 128–129, 132–133, 145, 148–149, 150, 154–155, 160, 161, 162, 164, 165, 166, 167, 170–171, 214–215, 222, 230, 231, 232–233, 234, 240, 251

The author owes a particular debt of gratitude for kindness and assistance over a period of many years to William Chaikin of Avco-Embassy, John Flinn at Columbia, Bob King and Leonard Shannon at Disney, Richard Kahn and Don Morgan at MGM, the indefatigable Bob Goodfried of Paramount, Jonas Rosenfeld, Bob Dengillian and Jet Fore at Twentieth Century-Fox, Lloyd Leipzig and Melinda Mullen at United Artists, Orin Borsten at Universal, and Bill Latham of Warner Brothers.

The independent publicists who, like their studio counterparts, increasingly perform as news bureaus for their films and clients, rather than as concocters of stunts and fabrications, are without number. My special thanks go to Rupert Allan, Ernie Anderson, John Blowitz, Arthur Canton, Warren Cowan, Mickey Freeman, Renee Furst, Margaret Gardner and David Golding in London, Dick Guttman, Al Horwits, Rick Ingersol, Frank McFadden, Roy Smith, John Springer, John Strauss and Ray Stricklyn, among many others.

I have skimmed the index and counted more than 300 names of those I have conversed with and in most cases interviewed and written about. They are the real sources for this book (freed, naturally, of all responsibility for anything I've said) because they have lived these movie and television years and have shared their experiences and insights with me. I am grateful to all of them and to all their colleagues who are not cited in the text but who have been no less generous with their time and thoughts.

I owe a very special note of appreciation to Annette Welles, at whose urging the book was contemplated and begun in the first place.

The picture researches were energetically pursued by Jean Acheson and James Pickett, and I thank them both. Thank you also Audrey Malkin, Librarian, Theatre Arts Library, UCLA, George Vescio of CBS, Earl Ziegler of NBC, Adrian Gould of KCET, Laurie Winfrey of *Newsweek, Books* and Sam Gill of the Margaret Herrick Library, AMPAS, for your kind and patient assistance in the search for appropriate illustrative material.

The typescript and index were prepared by Calliope, Inc. and for grace under terrible deadline pressure I am very grateful to Pat Hilton, Marilyn Baxter, Craig Marks and their other colleagues.

At Ward Ritchie, the enthusiastic and efficient support of the editor, William Chleboun, and the head of production, Ann Harris, have been all an author could ask. Not least of all do I admire their choice of Einar Vinje as book designer.

Final words of thanks are certainly due Alfred Hitchcock for that tasty Foreword; Jean Sharley Taylor and my other friends at the *Los Angeles Times;* and my family, for the patient forgiveness this project has asked of them.

Index

The numbers in boldface refer to photographs.